MW00426608

SPEAKING TUNISIAN:

A Love Story with Recipes

For Ali, omri

Contents

*"Out beyond ideas of wrongdoing
and rightdoing there is a field.
I'll meet you there.*

*When the soul lies down in that grass
the world is too full to talk about."*

- *Rumi*

PROLOGUE

A two-and-a-half-year-old girl twirls around the stone fountain which marks the center of the *piazza* in a small town of northern Italy. Her leather sandals slap the cobblestones beneath her feet, and her blue cotton dress swirls into the shape of a bell as she spins. Her straight blond hair and blue-green eyes make a stark contrast with the black hair and deep brown eyes of the other children around her, but she doesn't notice. *Ma come balli bene bella bimba, bella bimba, bella bimba...* Delighted with the sounds, she takes one of them as her new name. Biba.

A somewhat insecure adolescent with long legs and pimples saves her own life by auditioning for the LaGuardia School of the Performing Arts and moving to NYC from the suburbs of eastern Long Island. She finds herself happily surrounded by unique individuals, different in all kinds of ways. She takes an after-school job in a Chelsea diner to earn some pocket money.

A young American woman, living in Germany, arrives in

Paris for the first time. She walks out of the train station and is struck by the feeling that she has come home. Within weeks, she has packed up her Munich apartment, enrolled in the University of Paris, and quit her job as a dancer. Now in Paris, she takes a job in the Amex Café, the hub of the school, to balance the academic work and supplement her savings. She makes sandwiches, serves espresso and beer on tap to professors and students, thereby enjoying a growing circle of friends.

Arriving at JFK in NYC just before Christmas, a fresh graduate wearing a short bob, red lipstick, and a black turtleneck sweater, is informed at passport control that if she attempts to leave the country again before completing her jury duty, she will be arrested. A short holiday visit is extended another six weeks.

Waiting to perform her civic duty, this same young woman picks up a few shifts in a new restaurant recommended by a friend who works near NYU. On her first day, the owner shows her around. From a small huddle of kitchen staff, the owner's twin brother, tall and lithe, emerges in a chef's coat. He extends his hand. She looks up to meet the direct and inquisitive gaze of his coal-black eyes. This is where our story begins.

Habiba. Beloved.

THE TAILOR'S SHOP

On our first trip to Tunisia, I accompany my husband Ali on his daily tour. First order of business: Mouldi's tailor shop. Mouldi is Ali's best friend and former tailor master, a few years his senior. His tiny shop is situated on a main commercial street, sandwiched between a café and a dentist's office. This is the neighborhood where Ali grew up, and on the way we are stopped at every corner to exchange kisses and greetings with acquaintances, neighbors, distant relatives. «*Aslemma! Shnah'oulek? Le bes? Ommuk le bes? Buk le bes? Ouled le bes? Hamdullah!*" Good day! What's new? Everything OK? Your mother's OK? Your father's OK? Children OK? Thank God! How is life in the US treating us? Are we here for the summer?

We are in the heart of the neighborhood called Bab Menara, in the *medina*, the Arab quarter. Most of the families in this neighborhood have been here for generations and take a certain degree of pride in their citizenship. It is not a wealthy area, but its history is rich. Most of the buildings date from well before the arrival of the French colonists in the late 19th century.

While Ali gets caught up in jubilous reunions, I am transported by the sounds of the Tunisian language. I've heard him speak his native tongue, though it's possible I haven't really listened this closely before. At work, I have sometimes tried to follow Ali's conversations with his twin brother, gleaning meaning from the expressions on their faces, the mood afterward, or Ali's colorful and animated translations. But this is the first time I've really listened *in situ*, the language and its environment perfectly matched. What I hear doesn't resemble anything I know; voluptuous and sibilant sounds are perforated with guttural and percussive accents. The voices rise and fall in a cadence that, along with the expressions that light up their faces, suggests open emotional reveal. If I close my eyes, I hear the sound of fire; life-sustaining but also dangerous, mercurial, illuminating, and consumptive all at once.

I take in our surroundings. The buildings are small, inviting, sandwiched together. Here, in the *quartier arabe*, they are made of brick and stone, concrete, plaster, and are generally not more than a couple of stories high. The flat facades are whitewashed and show traces of neglect, like a favorite sweater one hasn't time to mend. These are punctuated by decorative wrought-iron window guards that billow out like pears. Both protective and welcoming, they curl like baroque embellishments, painted an enticing shade of blue. This blue is the color of the Tunisian summer sky that domes invitingly above me. It calls out brightly from doors and delivery trucks and store signs. It is Tunisia's hallmark color and only slight variations are tolerated.

Some of the finer houses boast a second story *ghenereya*, a squared off bay window, shuttered with intricately woven wooden screens that in days past enabled the ladies of the house to observe the comings and goings of the street below without being seen. A few of these *ghenereya* are painted blue or a deep forest green, but others are simply finished with a dark stain. Here and there, determined weeds, some with bright yellow flowers, burst through cracks in the plaster, reaching for the sun. The enormous, heavy arched doors, also blue or sometimes ochre-yellow, are decorated with big, black iron nails. The nails make connect-the-dots patterns of arrows and zigzags or more vegetal curls, and appear along with stylized fish or hands of Fatima, which provide protection for those who dwell within. Big black hammered-iron rings serve as knockers. Oftentimes, a smaller door is cut within the larger door, and the ancient proportions make it necessary for us to stoop when we enter.

From relatively simple exteriors we pass into foyers boisterous with decoration. Walls and floors, benches and stairs are covered with small tiles, hand-painted with wonderful geometric and floral motifs and blazing with pigments; ochre and brick red, forest green and every shade of blue from cobalt to palest sky. A potted succulent stands guard in the corner. To come from the stark white glaring sun outside into this cool, cloistered interior with all of its lively detail is truly a surprise and a delight. The thick stone walls shut out noise and heat, and we are invited, through all of our senses, to rest a while.

Generally, though, we can stay only for a brief exchange, and we continue on our pilgrimage. The streets are uneven, many still paved with cobblestones. They are narrow, designed for pedestrians and donkey carts, and as we pass the red doors of the *hammam*, we flatten ourselves against the wall so as not to get run over by a dented yellow taxicab. Feral cats slink around corners or shade themselves under parked cars. Women, draped in white *sefsersi*, push by on their way to market. These sari-like outer garments cover them from head to toe, giving the women a mysterious air of benevolent spirits as they float along the street. Dashing young men with gleaming hair whiz by on dilapidated motorbikes. The high-pitched whine of their approach, like the drone of an angry insect, sends everyone to the wall again, much to the young men's delight. Shopkeepers stand in the thresholds of their stores, assessing the qualities of the day that might influence their business: heat, dust, movement of air, density of pedestrian traffic, and another more elusive quality, unnamable, but important to consider nonetheless.

Mouldi's tailor shop is a sight to behold. A window and a door, both painted Tunisian blue, take up its entire facade. It bears no identifying sign. Inside, it is dark and cramped, maybe 12 square-feet total. Clothes are everywhere, hanging from nails on the wall, draped over chairs, in piles upon the table. A few old newspapers and plastic bags peek out here and there, empty water bottles, unwashed coffee glasses. A tiny ladder leads past a table with an ancient sewing machine to a tiny loft where the apprentices used to work. It is hard to imagine my 6' tall husband ever having been slight enough to fold himself into that space. Underneath the loft is a counter where Mouldi greets his customers and irons the finished clothes. He stands there now, baste-stitching a hem, a loose thread hanging from his lips. He looks at us over his glasses, and his serious, alert face breaks into a grin. I see a distinguished looking man in his early fifties, very slender, casually dressed in a collared shirt, summer slacks, and leather sandals. His large head is nearly bald, and he wears a closely manicured beard peppered with white. Over time I will come to know him as a true friend; patient, discerning, and immeasurably generous. He will serve as ambassador to our family in Tunis and contribute countless efforts on our behalf during periods of illness-- first Ali's mother's and then his father's. Later, he will single handedly supervise the construction of our house.

He ceremoniously clears one of the two chairs reserved for guests. These are always filled with friends; a dentist, a doctor

turned farmer, a former national judo champion turned farmer. It is, like many small businesses in Tunisia, a meeting place
where commerce and pleasure intermingle. Mouldi goes to the
café and returns with small, sturdy glasses of mint tea and coffee. My husband and his oldest friend will spend the next hour
talking of business and politics, family matters and local news.
Visitors will join in the conversation as they pass by. I will sip my
tea as I take in the atmosphere of congeniality among men while
the swallows dip and swoop across the sky outside the window.

SPEAKING TUNISIAN

At some point, after many such tours, I tired of being the only woman in the group and of trying to keep up with the conversation. The talk would inevitably slip from French, which they spoke in deference to me, back into the Tunisian dialect of Arabic. The latter was better suited to the subjects they were discussing, as well as to their passionate opinions about them. I had picked up enough of my husband's native language to know that the topics, which mainly centered around commerce, politics, and soccer, were not among my favorites.

In this way, I eventually came to take my place in the kitchen, surrounded by the women of the family: my mother-in-law, Zina, and her five grown daughters: Affifa, Raifa, Latifa, Mediha and Suaad. Theirs was a completely different society and atmosphere from that of the men. As important and cherished as they are, husbands and sons are generally exiled from the home until two o'clock, when the midday meal is served. Until then, the women run the ship, plan the meal, go to market, clean the house, wash the clothes, tend to the smaller children and the aged, and prepare tantalizing food.

Here, I discovered, was where the action was. The kitchen served as the turbulent yet ordered epicenter of the family. The women talked and laughed while they worked, told stories and teased each other, sometimes argued heatedly, their sharp voices slicing through the air. There was an unmistakable hierarchy, yet everyone participated more or less equally. There was a freedom of expression and a physical ease not as evident in the company of the men. The mood was festive, industrious, and tender. Unruly hair escaped from colorful headscarves and loose skirts or the *jelaba* got tucked unabashedly into undergarments while they did the laundry or washed the floor, leaving bare legs and feet exposed to welcome splashings of cool water.

With newspapers spread out on the floor, crouching on heels or sitting tailor-style in a circle, we peeled and pared vegetables and dropped them into great bowls of water, in preparation for the *cous-cous*, or the *tagine* of the day, or for one of many different kinds of salads. The women rhythmically ground garlic and herbs to a paste in the *meherez*, a heavy, brass mortar and pestle. The clinking and thumping created a sound to rival the *darbouka* - Tunisia's traditional drum - and the echoes could be heard from the kitchens of neighboring households, revealing the calm or agitated state of the cook.

All four of the stove's burners, lit with nearly empty disposable lighters from which only my sisters-in-law could manage to coax a spark, were constantly in use. Enormous pots, most of them severely dented and missing at least one handle, steamed away, precariously perched. From the earliest hour, the radio played popular European top 40's, as well as the latest Lebanese and Egyptian hits. One or more of the teenage nieces was always singing along, mirroring the vibrato and expressions of pain and despair they'd seen on TV. Neighbors, mostly women, inevitably stopped by for a coffee and a quick hello on their way to run an errand. They always shared some bit of news for the sisters to chew over long after the visitor had gone on her way.

I was eager to step into this circle but had been assigned the role of pampered and passive guest, a European woman who was probably unfit for the kind of work they were doing. Eventually I managed to convince them that it was a great deal more fun for me to help in the kitchen than to sit in the living room waiting for Ali to return.

Only two of my sisters-in-law spoke French, so it was imperative that I learn some Tunisian. The kitchen provided the perfect opportunity, and as we worked, I would point and ask "*Shnoua hedeka?*" What's this? Pepper: *fil fil*. Tomato: *t'matem*. Onion: *psall*. Cucumber: *farkouss*. Olive: *zitouna*.

Tunisian Arabic is often criticized in the Arab world for its impurities. This minuscule country was invaded and occupied by the Vandals, Romans, Turks, and the French, to name a few. An historically coveted mercantile port, Tunis (Roman Carthage) sits on the northern coast of Africa, sandwiched between Algeria and Libya. A ferry can take you across the Mediterranean Sea to Sicily in about six hours. As a result, its citizens are of every race, and each aspect of Tunisian culture reflects this diversity, including the language. I instantly recognized many words; *Farghitta* (fork) and *macroona* (macaroni) come from Italian, and the months of the year are only slightly different from the French. Other names had no relationship to anything I knew, leading to frequent confusion and hilarity; *Thum* (garlic), *atham* (eggs) and *thau* (light) proved particularly entertaining as I struggled to find the appropriate word. To this day I am likely to confuse *Sbah'al'chir*, which we use for good morning (it literally translates to "may your day be full of God's abundance"), with *Tisbah-alla-chir*, for good evening ("may you awake to God's abundance"), and am always dutifully and politely corrected by one of our nieces.

Learning Tunisian in this way, I was able to endear myself to my wonderful new relatives. Assumptions gradually melted as we came to know each other, and we grew to feel that there was not such a great difference between us after all. Over time and with many meals I became part of the family, an honorary *Tunsiya*.

FIVE SENSES

A week into my first trip to Tunisia, I suffered a kind of sensory overload. I had lived in a few different countries, including Germany, France and Italy, and adapted easily to different circumstances, but Tunisia was in an entirely different category. First of all, it was poorer than any country I had ever visited. There were sanitary conditions I had never before encountered. There was a sharpness, too, of character, a capacity for passions of all kinds, exacerbated by heat and lack. I had experienced something similar in Greece, and in Naples, many years ago, in certain neighborhoods. But this felt different, bringing to mind the stories of *A Thousand and One Nights* or the magic realism of Gabriel Garcia Marquez.

And then the brutal heat from the sun affected everything, intensifying and highlighting sights, smells, even sounds. In the bright light, people and objects seemed chiseled out against the white and turquoise blue background of the buildings; a myriad of faces, so many expressive and piercing eyes gazing intently, unabashedly into mine. In the markets, vendors offered their marinated olives in scruffy plastic bins, and baskets overflowed with a variety of herbs and spices, mounds of intense golden yellow and scarlet. I saw mountains of aromatic fruits, enticing though often unfamiliar. The cacophony of colors and shapes in the *souk,* along with the less subtle hawking of artisan wares in multiple languages, beckoned passersby.

And the smells could actually interrupt conversation.

Unpleasant smells - garbage dumped openly on the street corner, to be shoveled up and wheel-barrowed away at dusk; imperfect or hastily-built sewage conduits; cow and goat innards, displayed for sale at the market in an open plastic tub; body odor, unmasked or veiled with cheap perfume sold by the ounce from recycled whiskey bottles decorated with the labels of the brand names they imitated.

Of course there were enchanting smells, too: the spice vendor, with his big, burlap bags filled with mountains of cumin, coriander, mint, and 10 different kinds of paprika, wafting together to perfume the air in a wide circumference around his store; those same spices, circulating through the house as the family dinner simmered on the stove; the smell of fresh herbs growing in the driest of conditions and releasing their perfume with a gentle caress of the hand; the smell of frankincense and amber smoking on the *canoun* in the morning; and at night, the jasmine flowers, cascading down garden walls, releasing their scent into the evening air to mingle with that of the other evening-blooming perfumes.

After the first few days, even the passive act of listening to the language felt exhausting. The combination of unfamiliar, harsh syllables and the shouting, especially at family gatherings when 20 or 30 people of all ages are often competing for center stage, sent my head spinning. My first impression was one of great, boisterous celebration, but I wasn't used to it. Plus, we—my husband, his family, and myself—lived crowded into a relatively small apartment in the old part of the city, with vespas screeching around the corner on cobblestone streets just outside our window. Oftentimes during the summer, the sound of a wedding celebration fills the air, with its traditional *mizouit* band, consisting of a violin or lute, a bagpipe, and no fewer than three drummers. A wedding rarely winds down much before 3am. There was no escape.

The tastes, though, perhaps struck me the most. Anything required to grow under those conditions – 100+ degree heat for over 5 months of the year, beating sun, very little water - has to be strong. And the flavors were so intense, a highly-concentrated version of their American counterparts. The celery, for example, was thin, scrawny, a dark green, and so bitter it could only be used as an herb cooked in soups. Cucumbers grew thin, long and curved, and were covered with a dark, fuzzy skin that had to be scraped off. Carrots no bigger than my thumb and of a pale peach color packed the sweet flavor of fifteen of the vegetable of the same name back home. There were so many spices that I didn't recognize, so many new tastes to learn, and mealtimes generally offered a selection of five or ten different dishes. I wanted to try everything.

I quickly became overwhelmed. After five days, I felt dizzy and nauseous and had to retire to a cool, dark room and drink only water. "Sunstroke" was the verdict, although some suspected I was pregnant. I was of nervous temperament, they diagnosed--perhaps a tad sensitive in nature. My mother-in-law prescribed orange blossom water, which she doused over my head, and when that didn't work, she tried spearmint water, which did. It cut right through and cleared my senses, like smelling salts. After a brief respite of two days, I found myself able to rejoin the company and reacquaint myself with the various elements of what would become, with time, an intimately familiar and beloved culture.

ALI

Long after I have put the day to rest and fallen into a deep sleep, my husband comes to bed. It must be around 1AM as he crawls under the covers in the dark, careful not to wake me. I am aware of his presence nonetheless, and in half-slumber, I turn and wrap my arms around him, touch his face like a blind person, assessing his mood. My fingers flutter over a new pattern of clean-shaven skin and carefully decoupaged facial hair-soul patch, budding mutton chops. This is a new look for Ali, and I sit bolt upright in bed. I know what this means. He has decided to embark on a new business. We will be moving forward with the purchase of the old bakery.

In recent years, the selling of the restaurant and the opening of a pizzeria, both of them big, life-altering business decisions, were accompanied by dramatic changes in Ali's hairstyle. When we sold the restaurant, he let his hair grow, Samson-style, raising eyebrows and prompting concerned questions from customers and family - is everything ok with you and Ali? What's with the hair? In Tunisia that same summer, facing the prospect of a new enterprise, a life-long dream of making pizza, he emerged from the barber, a childhood friend, shorn close, his soft, tight, black curls left on the barber shop floor. No announcement, no public discussion, just the execution of a decision that had ripened and come to fruition.

We have been together for well over 20 years now, and I feel the word 'marriage' no longer suffices to describe our relationship. We have come to know each other in a way that would have been impossible without the many challenges we've faced, and without our distinctly different personalities, experiences, and cultural backgrounds.

Ali is larger than life, my Zorba, alternating between ringmaster and *boddhisattva*, between punishing work hours and completely unburdened repose, between rigorous discipline and bacchanalian sensuality. His relationships with family and close friends are marked on both sides by gestures of unfathomable generosity alternating with periods of contention that might last years. I have come to understand these relational mysteries as distinctly Tunisian, a by-product of what traditional Chinese medicine would identify as the fire element: passion and intensity, heat that warms and protects, but also curls and consumes, leaving ashes that nourish new growth.

At one point during my yoga teacher training, one of the students asked our teacher how she had found her guru. The guru, a Buddhist monk, had enjoyed a successful career as a university professor and had discovered the contemplative life relatively late in years. He was well versed in the scriptures, having completed the education of a Lama, and yet was able to communicate the principles of Buddhism in ways that any inquisitive modern person could understand. He cut a striking figure, a strapping, Irish-American in saffron robes, very engaging and charismatic. My yoga teacher explained the meaning of 'guru' as one who removes the darkness, allowing you to see the light, and furthermore, that it is traditionally the disciple, the seeker, who identifies and chooses his or her own guru. A guru can be an established and practiced teacher, but can also be a shoemaker, a grandmother, or a gardener. If this person gives you access to insights, if they, by example and from direct experience, guide you from blindness to clarity, then this is your guru.

My teacher then made one disclaimer: this is the rule as it applies if you are celibate and have chosen the spiritual path. If, however, you have chosen a committed partnership, marriage, family, then your guru is your spouse, and you are his or hers. Your family is the ground from which your spiritual awakening will unfold. All of the trials and tribulations of life as part of this family unit will be the equivalent of the challenges and tasks the guru assigns on the path toward enlightenment. A monk might command his disciple to sort grains of sand, light from dark, a seemingly punishing exercise in futility, testing the disciple's patience, resolve and faith. In a marriage, the equivalent becomes the negotiations over who does which chores, or where to celebrate Thanksgiving, when to find a new home, or how to discipline the kids. One partner might be fully committed to the Republican party, a lover of football and heavy metal, the other a Democrat who loves classical music, poetry, movies. This is fertile ground for spiritual transformation, for sure. Trial and error. *Rajas*, sustained effort. *Tamas*, receptivity and awareness. Compromise, compassion, self-reflection, forgiveness. *Sattva*, peace and equanimity.

This idea allowed me to appreciate my marriage in a completely different light. Like any couple, we have had multiple disagreements and tensions, stressed to capacity by children (5) and businesses (2, then 3, then 2) that consumed our energy, consciousness, our courage, our breath. Oftentimes, we felt separate in our struggles-- he with the challenges of the businesses; I with family and home. Our relationship has evolved over time, nourished by mutual admiration in our work life, curiosity about the world, passionate romance, the blessing of our big extend-ed family, and an indelible connection that seems mysterious, marked by the hand of destiny. Like most couples, we have also experienced moments of profound doubt and isolation, feelings of not being understood by the other, a sense of fatigue and futil-ity in our life as a couple.

Our schedules were opposite for the most part. I woke early with the kids and went to bed at nine after a joyfully exhausting day of keeping them fed, clean, and safe and, later, tending to their education. I did the bookkeeping when I could, made calls when there were issues that required negotiation, re-scheduled health department hearings during school hours. Ali, on the oth-er hand, slept until 10, went to market for miscellaneous items, then to the restaurant to receive and check all of the deliveries - fish from Capricorn, meat from Ottomanelli's, produce from Baldor's – then he went to look in on the Muffins Shop café, then back to the restaurant to supervise prep for the dinner service, and, finally to preside over the evening which began at 5pm - Showtime! He rarely made it home before midnight.

At home I was deprived of the fine dining and this came as a shock at first. For starters, I didn't know the first thing about how to prepare a meal! I could boil water for pasta and make scrambled eggs. I made good salads and baked a decent straw-berry-rhubarb pie, Ali's favorite. But nothing I tried came close to the sumptuous meals to which I (and the kids) had become accustomed. So in between his restaurant tasks, he taught me to cook by phone that first year of Epices.

I would tell him what I wanted to make, and he would give me the shopping list, with annoyingly thorough advice regarding color, texture, seasonal availability, size, etc. "Call me back when you have everything in the kitchen!" he would say. Then came the instructions on washing, peeling, chopping, size, color, shape, which knife, pan, etc. "Call me back when you have everything ready to go!" Finally, the instructions on cooking, one step at a time. These needed to be followed absolutely precisely. In the order given. No modifications. Temperature, flame, stirring or not stirring, color of browned meat, translucence of onions, everything fully described so that I could imagine him cooking there beside me. It was not unusual for there to be countless interruptions, either because he was at work or because I was with the children. Still, eventually, a final phone call would have him asking....,"So?!...How did it turn out?!" And I always knew he would love it. Even though his sous-chefs held their breath when he came to taste their preparations, I never worried that he would reprimand me. He was so happy to share his knowledge, and he always complimented me on my efforts, even when I made mistakes.

For the most part, though, our moments together were scattered and unpredictable. I would frequently awake when he came home, nurse the baby and then sit with him while he down-shifted from the busy evening to the peace and comfort of the nest. At this late hour, and to my surprise and delight, he would eat the leftovers from our dinner, too agitated and adrenaline-pumped to eat at the restaurant with the staff at 10.30-- and happy to enjoy the fruits of our cooking lesson. We would discuss the newsworthy events of the day or, more often, open the floodgates and release hours, sometimes days, of pent-up frustration and doubt, triumph and delight. I would share the children's antics, which simultaneously exasperated and entertained. I would confess insecurities about mothering and never having a moment's peace. He would tell me about the sharks that circle every business, the employees for whom he carried a deep sense of personal responsibility, and whose interpersonal conflicts and professional quirks simultaneously exasperated and entertained. In a way, we had the same complaints, but could do little to ease each other's burdens because we were fully occupied and tethered by our own. Somehow during those years we each discovered and adopted a symbolic gesture toward the other. I would often wake to a beautiful bouquet of flowers on the dining room table. He would wake most mornings to his tea, boiled until it resembled coffee, dark and strong, just the way he liked it.

Oftentimes, I would pack everyone up and go to Epices for a family dinner. When the kids were little we would come on a Monday or Tuesday, so as to profit from the slower business and Ali's relative freedom to sit with us. Later, when Aziz was in grade school around the corner from the restaurant, we would go to the park after school, or to the Natural History Museum a few blocks north if the weather was unfavorable. We would play and then come back to the restaurant to eat, sometimes early on a Friday, so that we could put off the homework that was due on Monday and sleep late on Saturday. We tried as best we could to introduce a semblance of order into what seemed on most days like rampant, albeit lively, chaos.

As the kids grew and were doled out to pre-school or to accompany Papa on an errand, I gradually resumed more of the administrative tasks I had given up when they were babies. Ali was happiest when we were around, close enough to come and kiss, but out of his hair when the heat was on. He was a master of incorporating family and work, but at times I found this insanely challenging. If the kids were fussing I wanted nothing more than to be home, in my quiet living room, softly singing to them as they dropped off to sleep. But we lived in Inwood, an hour away from the restaurant by subway. So instead I had to take them around the block in the stroller or carrier. Or I tried to recreate the atmosphere of home in the cramped basement office with a bassinet, a makeshift bed, both with blankets that smelled familiar, and a table lamp instead of the neon lights that normally glared overhead. Later, we rented a tiny apartment/office where we put a mattress in the loft. This provided some relief, giving us a place to retire as homework, naptimes, and mealtimes modulated and transformed with the children's steady evolution.

We made so many adjustments just to be near Ali, but for the most part it was better than being at home without him and far from the action. Besides, he made it totally worth our while to stay. He was, and still is, charismatic and unpredictable in the most delightful ways. He took us on spontaneous trips to Chinatown to repair a toaster or to purchase a new piece of equipment for the kitchen, introduced us to the street vendors in the neighborhood, patient sellers of used books, handbags or hats, fruit or African sculptures.

Many had become his devoted friends. Each one in turn had exchanged stories with him. They came from Bangladesh or Pakistan or Kenya, fellow immigrant-merchants in the melting pot of their chosen home of NYC. They found comfort in sharing the tales of their struggles back in their homelands. Whether they left for political or economic reasons, they shared the urgent need to leave a beloved country in which poverty or annihilating violence were certainties for anyone who stayed. They all shared stories of how they had formed an exit plan which then led to the fresh hardship of travel fraught with danger and risk. Tremendous faith and courage were needed and finally, hopefully, good fortune, the grace of finding seasoned immigrants from home who had come before and could offer guidance, maybe even a starting point. Or perhaps the chance stumbling upon a big-hearted native New Yorker sympathetic to their plight who could offer them a job or temporary shelter.

For most, work came first, something steady if they were lucky. Romance and/or marriage came later, either with someone from a totally different culture or with someone from home if their papers were in order and they could afford to bring a bride from their native country. Either path was treacherous and steep. A cross-cultural relationship could be fraught with misunderstanding and power struggles. But bringing a bride from her native country to the US brought different challenges. For a woman who had lived a sheltered life, familiar only with the deep traditions of her people, adjusting to a culture in which tradition had little or no value could be heavy with grief and isolation. In the US, adaptation and resilience are the tools that guarantee success. Sometimes these women returned to their countries, unable to sustain the loneliness of living so far from their families and traditions. They preferred the depressed material circumstances of their native country to the harsh reality they discovered in the land of promise and plenty. Immigrant stories are often full of heartbreak.

Over the years, Ali has served as a guide to many of our immigrant friends. He chose a different culture and threw himself into his new life whole-heartedly, without ever forgetting his home, his Tunisian heritage. Within the five-block radius of the store, he is known and loved by nearly all of the merchants and many of the residents. To this day he lives with his feet firmly planted in the present but with a deep and reverent bow to his past, his culture, his birthplace. For me, too, his stories of Tunisia, his poetic explanations of traditions or beliefs, have offered guidance and a sense of rootedness very different from that of my European-American intellectual-bohemian childhood of the 70's. When I am lost in the fumbles of the past or the myriad possibilities of the future, he coaxes me back to the present moment. "What is most important right now?" he might ask, or more pointedly, "*Hata n'aichu*!!" (If we're alive tomorrow!).

When I complain of fatigue, his prescription is work, but work without resistance, with an inquisitive mind and a joyful attitude. "Peace, pace, and patience" is his favorite aphorism. Doing what he is supposed to do, as best he can, he says, has taught him everything he needs to know about life. That and an inherent curiosity about people and what makes them tick. Somehow people entrust him with their stories. They open to his inquisitiveness. They sense that he will cater to the best in them, even when he understands their weaknesses. Working by his side has taught me about compassion, relinquishing personal agendas and self-righteousness in favor of a connection made in service to another.

When I am picking at the lint on our complex and ever-changing life quilt, honing in on the blemishes, he reminds me of our many blessings, the richness and beauty of the quilt itself. Over the years, as I have studied meditation and the spiritual practices of yoga and Buddhism, sought guidance in Sufism and the poetry of Rumi, he has always invoked parallels in the words of his mother. When I came to him from a class discussion on *pratipaksha bhavana* - the practice of tilting a perception from negative to positive - he compared it to something he had learned as a child. If he or his siblings came downstairs in the morning with a scowl on their faces, his mother would tell them to be thankful for the blessing of another day and to say good morning, even if they didn't feel like it. In the same way, at night in bed, in the spacious moment before sleep, she would invoke gratitude again, work laid to rest, no matter what burrs still lay under the skin. Thank You, I am many times blessed. *Hamdullah.*

As a twin, as one of three brothers and five sisters, Ali has had his share of competing for scarce resources. He is generous where he perceives a need. Some of the least fortunate in the neighborhood are also some of our most loyal customers. Ali always informally extends them credit when they are down and out at the end of the month, counting the steps to payday. Other customers, having forgotten their wallets, or realizing too late that they have insufficient cash, have been given their completed order nonetheless, in a gesture of trust generally unheard of in NYC. Ali tells them they can pay next time, and they always do.

In the beginning of our business life together, we had debt hovering over us and young children needing food and shelter. Optimizing the profit margin was imperative. Back then, this practice of his tested my tolerance for risk and strained my patience. Ali explained that in his thinking, one of two things would happen: either the customer was a crook who would gloat over his free meal for a day, never to return for fear of being remembered, or else he was honest and would remain a faithful customer for life because he had been treated like a friend. Ali banked on the latter and, indeed, we enjoy to this day a plethora of loyal, contented customers who feel like friends.

When we first met, ages ago, he was married, his wife on maternity leave with their second child. I was enjoying what I thought would be a brief interlude from the home I had made for myself in Paris. I was moonlighting as a barista in the restaurant Ali's brother had opened and for which Ali had set up the kitchen, created the menu and was training the staff. For two months we worked as colleagues, enjoying a seamless and utterly platonic working relationship. I had it in my mind to return to Paris as soon as I completed my jury duty. He, on the other hand, intended to return to Montreal once the restaurant was running smoothly. He had been the head chef for ten years at an acclaimed restaurant in Montreal until it was sold.

By March, both of us had returned to our respective countries without a second thought. He was in Montreal with his young family, looking for work, while I was in Paris with my best friend, working in a restaurant, harboring vague ideas of finding and marrying a jazz musician and figuring out what to do with my life for the umpteenth time. If we thought about each other at all, it was with the respect of one colleague for another. We had worked together in perfect synchronicity, a team of waitress and chef with the same work ethic, the same delight in a perfectly executed dinner experience.

By July of the same year, however, we had both returned to NYC, and to the restaurant. He had been unable to find work in Montreal and also unable to convince his wife to uproot and return with him to NYC. I had been unable to shake the feeling that my life was playing itself out back home, a place I had never included in my ruminations about the future. And there to ambush us upon our return was cupid's arrow; unmistakable and a complete surprise to us both, overwhelming and complicated and altering the course of our lives and the lives of those close to us. The rest, as they say, is history. Thirty years later we are still soulmates, business partners, sweethearts, and each other's gurus.

Of course, like any guru, any husband, any father, brother, son, like any human, he is a living consortium of perfect imperfections. He can galvanize people with his creativity and connection to life, but he also has his own conditions for a perfect storm. When fatigue, unreliable blood sugar, overload of work and/or family-related challenges and phases of the moon assemble in just the right configuration, his entire aspect darkens. His eyes and mouth drop almost imperceptibly. He will scan, in those moments, the immediate environment for the trigger factor that unleashes his fury. It might be a messy room, or food wasted, or a provocative response from someone he loves. Then we can all watch the swell of the wave as it rises, and we either hold fast or scatter for the discharge. The damage is never lasting, his bark worse than his bite, but the contrast is so stark, the darkness so dark. In those moments I try to remember not to yell back. I try to share what I have learned. I prepare his favorite dishes. And he does the same for me, when my moments of darkness appear.

As spontaneous and creative as he is, he can also freeze in the face of a major decision - opening or selling a business, moving to a new place and buying a house, any kind of uprooting, anything that might put at risk those who depend on him. He might experience a long stretch of discontent as he navigates uncharted territory. He needs to test the waters, jockey for position before he can shift from one boat to the other and we all set sail on a new voyage. He feels a tremendous amount of agitation during this process, which, to a great extent, he internalizes. Talking helps less in these moments of transition, although if I can manage to listen with an open heart, he will find his groove of purpose after sifting through and discarding multiple extraneous possibilities. Peace, Pace, Patience. Until then, I read his facial hair like a stargazer.

EPICES DU TRAITEUR

We opened our restaurant on October 21st, 1996, just days before our first born Aziz's first birthday. It had taken about four
months to complete the renovations, which included gutting and
cleaning the space; a long, narrow room with a garden in back
and a cramped basement accessible by a steep, narrow staircase.
Our address was just around the corner from the Muffins Shop,
our café of two years. Although on a side street, the restaurantt
was visible from Columbus Avenue, an important consideration
for the pedestrian traffic we hoped to attract. You had to go down
a few steps to enter the restaurant, and there was a small, gated
space in front that was just big enough for a small table or two on
balmy evenings.

With our limited budget and the pressure to open as soon as
possible, we focused on a few key components of the decor and
on building and equipping an efficient kitchen. We uncovered
what became an exposed brick wall and polished the hardwood
floor. We moved the bar, which had been in an awkward niche
just next to the entrance, to the front of the restaurant, to greet

customers as much as to pour wine and write out checks. The niche became the home of the coveted table number 1, a little alcove just big enough for one small table with three places. This alcove, visible from the street, offered the only semi-private dining in an otherwise railroad-style designed space where all the tables were next to each other like band musicians in long, neat rows.

The *piece de resistance*, however, was the facade. We revamped it in the spirit of the French *bistro*, with double French doors and an European awning. We painted the entire facade a bright, fire engine red, with the name hand-painted up above in gold and black lettering. The red paint prompted intense protest from our contractor, who had painstakingly attached molding to the facade, choosing wood to match that of the bar, which he had built to echo the lines and shapes of the facade. He was absolutely adamant about staining the wood the same tint inside and out. Ultimately we convinced him to see things our way by showing him pictures of French bistros from guide books and travel magazines. A few years later, the bistro style would become more popular in New York City, and our façade would become almost commonplace. We opened up the rear wall so that the kitchen could have the same open quality that had been such a part of Pamela's, his brother's restaurant. We also built a refrigerated salad bar in the back, covered in blue and white Mexican tiles, because we had planned to open for lunch as well as dinner and imagined this would be an important feature. Both these elements would be revisited and ultimately transformed as we grew to know our new business.

For decoration, we painted the walls a light yellow and displayed a collection of small, gilded mirrors my mother had amassed over the years from garage sales and given to us as an opening gift. Over the years we would add, among other things, an antique shelf and some plates from Tunisia, pig and fish nick-knacks, a Moroccan samovar, and a collection of miniature oil paintings of delicately executed vegetables, purchased from a local gallery whose owner we had befriended. Like the Muffins Shop, décor developed over time as we found things we could afford that delighted us, much in the way most of us decorate a home.

We scheduled opening night for October 21, 1996. Aziz was a few weeks shy of his first birthday, very active and vocal. My nearly full-time occupation was following him around to make sure he didn't get into mischief. On the side, I did the bookkeeping at the Muffins Shop, as well as all the paper work required to set up the restaurant. Nonetheless, I felt certain I'd be able to handle the additional work of hostess at our restaurant. After all, this was the culmination of our dream as a couple. We would be back to the working relationship that had started the whole thing. I had a babysitter lined up whose services would be shared with a close friend in the neighborhood. Three nights a week, I would bring Aziz over to her apartment at about 5pm. She was a single mom with a two-year-old daughter. Aziz already felt at home with them, and the arrangement suited her perfectly.

On opening night, though, we wanted him with us. He had been at our side nearly every day at the Muffins Shop from the time he was a newborn, after all. Nothing could have been more natural for us, or for our customers. As to the customers, we invited friends and supporters to join us for our grand opening. My dear friend Diane, whose family had helped us get our start, was there from Paris. We invited many of our suppliers, our fellow neighborhood merchants, our closest friends and relations; anyone who was at all connected to our family, to the Muffins Shop, who had been part of this substantial support network we felt holding us up, wishing us well. We had not yet received our wine and beer license but invited everyone to bring their own and invited them to their first meal at 'Epices', on the house.

Aziz was somewhat overwhelmed at the sheer quantity of people streaming in that evening. He clung to me like a little monkey, curious, but unwilling to relinquish the safety of my arms. About an hour into dinner, we realized that we were short-staffed in the dining room. The food was backing up in the kitchen. One customer perceived our moment of panic and offered his help. Pretty soon, the kitchen and dining room were full of customers pitching in, waiting and bussing tables. What could have been a disaster turned into a brilliant celebration of friendship. The atmosphere was one of a big family affair.

Months later, a friend and neighbor who had captured the event with photos brought over a lovingly assembled album; raised glasses, colorful plates heaped with *couscous, tagine, slata fakhous*, familiar faces laughing or discussing passionately, half-full glasses hovering over empty plates. And all throughout, Ali and I, Aziz on my hip, faces bright with delight, effort, surprise, relief, the launching of our dream.

HOME COOKING

Nana had six children in as many years; a girl, another girl, fraternal twin girls, and, finally, the dearly wished-for boys, identical twins. Shortly thereafter her husband, Meherez (known to us as Azizi, 'dear one'), an established florist, went blind from glaucoma. A last baby boy and a friend's orphaned daughter made eight children to feed and raise. Nana wasted little time on self-pity. She set to work training her eldest as mother's helpers, enlisted the aid of family and neighbors, and got a job as a nighttime patient care assistant in a hospital ward reserved for cognitively challenged children. In response to his wife's tireless encouragement, Azizi re-opened a tiny abandoned store that had been in her family for many years, filling it with household necessities; milk, eggs, soap. He familiarized himself with the feel of the different coins and, thrifty by nature, ran the store with only the occasional robbery, from 8am until 8pm for forty years thereafter.

The boys, charming and full of energy, were allowed to roam the neighborhood while the women cleaned and cooked.

They were reprimanded and punished for small but frequent infractions and often ushered home with stern admonitions to the parents to rein them in. Nana, who had received very little education, despaired when her sons did poorly in school. With a heavy heart, she decided to send them to a boarding school in a small country town called Zagouan, some four hours from Tunis. They remained there for eight years, coming home during the summers. Many years later, she confessed that her only regret in life was having sent them away. She blamed their emigration to America on that earlier separation.

When, years later, we would visit Nana and Azizi each July, the reunion was fraught with emotion, particularly between Nana and her sons. They would hug and weep, kiss and caress each others' faces and hands, taking in the changes of the past year. All of the sadness of those lost years, all of the longing and anxious waiting flooded the first moments of our arrival. Then we would make the rounds with kisses for everyone, followed by questions and stories over a big afternoon meal.

Before they were sent to boarding school, there was one year during which they went to school in Tunis. My husband tells of running up the cobblestone street toward their house and smelling dinner cooking even before they turned the corner into the entryway. Through the door they ran, and up the stairs to the kitchen where Nana was putting the finishing touches on the afternoon meal. She would sit them down and make them taste what was cooking on the stove. She often cooked up something new, conjured from the market's bountiful selection of produce and from her own special blends of spices, which had been dried on bed sheets on the roof and finely ground with the mortar and pestle.

The boys, cooped up in school all day, might have been anxious to change into their play clothes and run out into the street, but she would coax them into staying just a bit longer, urging them to taste again as she narrated her cooking. "This way, my sons, if you marry a woman who can't cook, you will not starve, and you will teach her!" I can imagine her, glad to have them home after the day's absence, sensing the speed with which they were growing, trying to stave off, with her lovingly prepared food, the driving restlessness that was already pulling them from her.

ICH'R YID

Friday is the day when Tunisians go visiting. They spend the morning praying in the mosque (typically the men), preparing the midday meal (women), eating together, and finally collapsing into siesta. In the late afternoon, one or two members of the family will venture out to visit a cousin, or a sister and her family, or an older relative, to cheer someone who is ailing or infirm. The rest will stay at home and receive any visitors who may appear.

None of this is pre-arranged and often two or three branches of the family will congregate at the same time. Greetings are exchanged, hugs and clusters of kisses, genuine and full of delight, or laced with decorum and shades of hypocrisy, or hesitant, a recent squabble still lingering. Children get passed around, necks craned, lips pursed like cherubs, from one auntie or aged unshaven uncle to the next. No one is spared.

Once everyone is seated in the living room or the courtyard, one of the aunties disappears into the kitchen and returns flushed with anticipatory pride or embarrassment, carrying trays of refreshments: sweet green tea with sprigs of fresh mint, steaming amber in tiny glasses ornate with gold filigree; *baklava* and little balls made from almond paste, colored pink and pistachio green and infused with the soapy, aromatic taste of scented geranium; cylindrical cookies, called *raïba*, made from roasted chickpea flour, that stick to the roof of the mouth like peanut butter; doughnut-shaped almond pastries, flavored with rose water and liberally dusted with powdered sugar; homemade syrupy-sweet lemonade or strawberry ices laced with orange blossom water. An uncle might give a child a couple of *dinar* to go to the corner store and purchase 200 mg paper cones of roasted almonds, roasted chickpeas, and *klub* - roasted sunflower seeds, black and piping hot. The hulls will be piled on the table cloth or scattered on the courtyard floor, to be swept up after the guests have gone.

While the smaller children chase each other or sneak forgotten sweets, the older children congregate just outside the door for an impromptu game of street soccer or to try on one or another of the hats of adolescence they have witnessed, safe from the disapproving glances of their parents, but close enough to feel protected should anything backfire.

Seldom are tremendous personal or intellectual revelations exchanged at these gatherings. They retain a formal aspect, despite the familiar surroundings and congenial atmosphere. Subtle inferences and attitudes are noted and set to marinate. Information is traded, health inquired after, news relayed of the successes and failures of family members who are not present, many living abroad. Here, the bonds of the family are strengthened, the shared values reiterated, as they respond in unison, *"Hamdullah!"* (Thank God!), or *"Lutuf, lutuf, lutuf!"* (Heaven forbid!) to accounts of fortunes, good and bad.

If the visit extends into the evening, or if visitors appear around mealtime, they are always invited to stay. Not to do so would be a blatant insult. This often means that we eat in shifts around the small, foldout dining table: children and old people first, then the men and the adolescents, then the women who have cooked the meal. The women have been tasting while cooking and are inevitably experts at sucking the meat from the bones and from the fish heads that remain.

Initially, the practice offended my western, feminist sensibilities. I felt it was sexist, the women meekly taking their place at the end of the family bread line, evidence of archaic patriarchal oppression. But over time, as with many things I witnessed in Tunisia, I have come to understand that things are not always what they seem. The women, at least in my family, would not take first pick even if it meant the choicest morsels. The bounty they reap at the end of the meal is so much greater. Here, they can eat and linger undisturbed, released from the impatient appetites of the rest of the family. The sorority that has carried them through the chores of the day finds its culmination here in celebratory indulgence. As they eat, they tell stories and laugh until they cry or choke, filling in the events of the day for a sister who came in at the end of the preparations, but who, nonetheless, claims membership to this privileged group.

Even if the meal has already ended, the dishes washed and put away, a latecomer is offered sustenance nonetheless. Places are set, leftovers heated. In a pinch, a can of tuna, some *harissa* mixed with olive oil, a boiled egg cut in four, a dish of olives, bread to eat it with, and a sweating bottle of water make a nice meal. *"Ich'r yid,"* Nana used to say. "You arrive just at the last bite", and food would be conjured from nothing, prompting indignant cries of protest from her children, who had just been chased out of the kitchen while looking for leftovers.

POMEGRANATE STORY

Because of the restaurant, our rendezvous are usually late. While most couples sleep, we steal a few uninterrupted moments, going over the events of the day. This is a wonderful time for both of us. Our various responsibilities are temporarily put to rest; the restaurant is closed, the children are asleep. Ali eats the dinner I've left for him on the stove, and afterwards he might light up his *houka*, filling the kitchen with its smell of apple-flavored tobacco. Oftentimes, he brings home a case of fruit, and we might prepare some as a late dessert or for the kids' breakfast. Mango or cactus fruit, peeled and cut, bowls of grapes or apples and pears, all washed. On this particular occasion, he comes home with a case of pomegranates.

Anyone who has tried it knows that preparing pomegranates is a labor of love. They seem to have been created specifically to discourage any attempt at extracting the plump, red seeds, which burst easily and must be handled with great care. The ruby seeds are packed tightly together in the skin of the fruit and need to be coaxed from the pith that holds them. Paper-thin membranes run throughout and also have to be removed with dexterous fingers. The juice inevitably splatters over clothing and countertop and stains fingertips a dark wine color for some time afterward. It might take twenty minutes to turn one fruit into a handful of ruby seeds, ready to eat. As we work, he tells me this story:

The pomegranates of his childhood were a winter fruit, associated with long, chilly afternoons inside with nothing to do, nowhere to go. His mother would summon everyone to help prepare two or three for a snack. They would tell stories or listen to the radio while they were working. Imagine the scene: everyone sitting around the gas space heater, shoulders hunched, hats and scarves on, bundled beneath layers of sweaters and socks to ward off the inevitable cold that seeps up through the carpet from the tiled floor. Moods and faces are grim so many hours before lunch or after dinner, until the talking begins, or a favorite Om Kalthoum song has everyone swooning.

The inner workings of relationships between the siblings rise to the surface, and quirks of personality come to light. Who enjoys the dexterous precision of cleaning the fruit but is indifferent to the taste? Who is too impatient or lazy to do the work but loves the sweet juice of the seeds? Who completes the chore dutifully yet sharply resents the sister who, free and easy, gives away the fruits of her labor to the last sister who always manages to wiggle out of the task?

Only Nana, the matriarch, saw and understood the intricacies, the subtle hierarchies and negotiations in the relationships between her daughters. She would mix the seeds with *z'har* (orange blossom water) or *atarsheiya* (geranium water) and heaping spoons of sugar. For each of her three sons, too young, too boisterous to participate, she would leave a small piece with the seeds still attached to the pith and a bit of the peel. For each of her little roosters, *serdouk*, a cock's comb.

32 SARDINES

Growing up in Ali's family home, it was the custom for one of the children to give up his bed if a relative came to stay for the night. On this particular occasion, little Mohamed had offered his bed to Abu Razzek, his father's brother. During the day, Nana had prepared a sumptuous dinner. With their limited means, she had decided on fresh sardines as the fish. Coated with a mixture of flour, cumin and garlic, sautéed in vegetable oil, they would be served with a mixture of fried potatoes, both *haar* (hot) and *halou* (sweet) fried peppers, and fried squash, all mixed together in a dish called *kefteji*. Soup, salad, and plenty of French bread would fill out the meal, but she was anxious it wouldn't be enough. She had counted out thirty-three sardines; three each for herself, her husband, their guest, and each of the eight children, now old enough to be perpetually famished. The food was ready well before the mealtime hour and, in the interim, one sardine mysteriously disappeared from the platter. She noticed its absence as she was about to bring the dish to the table and counted them again. Thirty-two sardines. Rather than make a fuss, she ate one less herself and said nothing.

The visit was a happy one and, at breakfast the next morning, she asked her brother-in-law how he had slept. "Pretty well, considering that the entire cat population of Tunis was under my bed, meowing the night through." Little Mohamed had hidden the stolen fish under his mattress, forgetting that he would not be sleeping in his own bed!

FAST FOOD

Ali and his brother used to come home stuffed to the gills from having gorged on street food. They would have earned a few *millimes* unloading a melon truck or standing watch over a store for fifteen minutes or delivering a package or a message in the neighborhood. Ravenous as only growing boys can be, they would head for their favorite *leblebi* or *mischoui* stand. There, they would purchase a snack with portions and ingredients far more generous than what their mother could afford. The chickpea soup, *leblebi,* garnished with beef hooves, an extra egg or tuna, as much bread and *harissa* as they could pack in. And the atmosphere of masculine appetite and banter satiated their maturing curiosity as well. *Mischoui,* or assorted grilled meats, offered an unimaginable wealth of carnivorous delights. Lamb chops, thinly sliced beef scallops, skewered kabobs, all seasoned with lemon juice, parsley, and chopped onion, served with copious amounts of bread, and a choice of salads: spicy *slata mischouia*, made from grilled peppers; *omuk houria,* a cooked carrot salad seasoned with cumin and garlic; *slata farkous,* made from chopped cucumbers and tomatoes with onion and fresh mint. Ali has taken us to eat at a few of these *mischoui* places. The smell is intoxicating and the atmosphere just what you would imagine: crowds of hungry people; greasy kitchens aflame with fiery cooks who move the meat with theatrical dexterity; no-fuss stainless steel or Formica tables and plastic chairs for easy cleaning; squares of newsprint paper to wipe your hands; a tiny, dirty sink to wash them after your meal. Often a full grown ram, alive and fierce, with impressive, curling horns, is tied to a nearby tree, advertising the establishment.

Other vendors offer fresh lemonade and *bambalone* (fried dough dipped in sugar) or cakey biscotti to dip in the sour-sweet drink. Tunisian lemonade is made from the entire lemon, which gives it a hint of bitterness, and is often flavored with orange blossom water, *z'har*.

Bakeries and pastry shops abound in an effort to satisfy the Tunisian sweet tooth. Traditional Arab pastries intermingle here with French *millefeuille* cakes or cheerful fruit tarts. Savory treats are often served on the go from separate windows: thin squares of pizza with tuna or anchovies & olives; a puff pastry treat filled with tuna and egg, misnamed *paté*; *brik* or *sweba fatima*, deep fried tuna and egg-filled, flaky phylo treats; and my favorite, the *fricass*ée, a small roll of fried bread into which has been unceremoniously stuffed just a little of each of the following: tuna, egg, potato, olive, onion, and *harissa*.

After a street food orgy, Ali and his brother would arrive home often just before mealtime and excuse themselves, begging off, so as not to hurt their mother's feelings, by telling her that they were tired or not feeling well. Years later, of course, it was their mother's cooking they dreamed of and which would inspire them to cook for others. The street food, though, still holds a certain charm, and we make a pilgrimage to his favorite haunts every time we are in Tunis. It's my turn now to receive my boys "not really hungry" for dinner, after an afternoon of errands in the city with their father.

DAR NANA

Aicha and I walk down the sloping cobblestone street of the *rue de la Riviere*, on our way to Mouldi's shop to pay our respects and whittle away the evening. We are escaping the cramped quarters of the apartment where we are staying with Azizi, where he and Nana lived the last fifteen years of her life and where she died two years ago. The day is hot, even though siesta has long passed, and a lazy quiet pervades. It will be more than a few hours before night falls and cools the air, before the citizens of Tunis find their second wind.

Nana and Baba's apartment has three windows, unusually large and protected from the outside by wrought iron cages painted turquoise-blue. On the windowsill, the dried-out vine from a potted jasmine plant struggles, winding its way through the blue curlicues toward the sky, where its few remaining delicate leaves will drink in the sun. The bold 1970's pattern of the orange and brown curtains is just visible from the street. The size of these windows belies the stark and cramped interior: two small bedrooms, a bathroom, and a tiny foyer, all open out onto to the sitting room. There is a minuscule kitchen to the right of the entrance, just off of the foyer. The ceilings are high throughout, but there is very little surface area and, when the numerous members of the extended family come to visit, traffic becomes a problem. You can see the children wishing they could will their kinetic little bodies to float up and play above the grownups, who sit squeezed together on the three sofas and talk endlessly. Besides the two windows that look out over the narrow street, there are small windows high up in the walls between the rooms. These were designed for air circulation but are ineffectual even when their shutters are kept wide open. Storage spaces are up there, too, accessible only with the aid of a ladder.

There have been times while visiting when I thought I would go mad in the restricted space, especially with my two young boys chasing each other in place and contributing great quantities of noise from which no one could escape. All of this was made doubly unbearable by the fact, known to all, that Nana had not always lived this way.

Zeineb ben Saad, known to us as Nana, used to live in a grand house. It was big enough for two families or more. As the first-born daughter in her family, she inherited the house, along with the little store around the corner, from her father. Hers was the third generation to own and inhabit it. She shared the upper floor with her younger sister, Mongeia, newly married at the time. The bottom floor was let out to another family, first to a cousin and her six children, then to two other consecutive tenants and their families. Uncle Hamaïs, a bachelor vagabond and Nana's youngest brother, would come and stay in between jobs, sleeping on a couple of sheepskins in the courtyard. Once her husband's income was established, Mongeia moved out with her family. Nana's first-born daughter, Affifa, married and started her family in the house, ushering in the fifth generation to live there.

By the time I came into the picture, they had sold the house, for reasons financial and personal, seeing no other solution to the hardships that plagued them at the time. The children were grown and married, and the only justification for keeping such a large house would have been sentimental attachment, a luxury they could not afford. But the stories about *dar Nana*, (Nana's house) abound, and I have heard many of them. Her home was a center of hospitality, of legendary all-nighters with laughter ringing throughout the neighborhood, and of fights, also legendary, generally finishing out a celebration of one kind or another. Nana's presence was ubiquitous, her vigilance and her compassion completely tied up with the place in which she had lived all her life.

The traditional house in the *medina* reveals little from the outside: a thick, whitewashed wall in a narrow alley, an impressive wooden door, a small window, shuttered or curtained. Only rarely does a slight breeze or someone's negligence afford a glimpse inside. The gaze rests for a moment, anticipating, and encounters a pair of eyes, rising to the challenge, a pair of forearms, folded over ample breasts, protective.

Nana's house had been built in the traditional, pre-colonial style, with separate rooms in a perimeter opening up onto a generous courtyard. On the second floor, more rooms above the ones below, opening onto a wrap-around balcony. Grainy, black and white family pictures give only glimpses of the courtyard and its lavish decoration. Antique tiles, one can only guess the colors – ochre and burnt orange, or aquamarine and deep indigo – cover the floor and the walls up as far as the eye can see. The patterns are more intricate than the ones we see today, more carefully drawn. Seemingly delicate marble columns are visible, and cheerful, heavy curtains billow at the entrances to the rooms.

One can just make out a young fig tree close by the well.

My husband used to tell me how, on scorching summer nights, everyone would pull their mattresses out of the rooms, onto the balcony. If there was a full moon, Nana was careful to hang makeshift drapes to protect her sleeping children from the harmful rays that might cause mysterious illness or even insanity. In the winter time, during siesta, she would lay herself down at the entrance to the room her sons shared. Certain of their intention to sneak out and explore once she had fallen asleep, she positioned herself as a living security system. No one could leave or enter without waking her. No one dared.

During times of financial strain, Nana would sell one or two of the family heirlooms that had come with the house: gold bracelets from her mother's dowry; valuable vases or framed Koranic scripture, embroidered in gold on black velvet; hand woven kilims of brightly colored wool from the desert nomadic traditions of the South; silver tea sets with brass inlay. Her family's artisanal trade had been the making of *shesheiya*, the cylindrical, bright red felt hats worn by men, sometimes adorned with a long, black, silk tassel. The *shesheiya* craftsmen had special status. Their work didn't made noise like the artisans who hammered designs into copper plates, nor did it give off an odor like the leather craftsmen. Because of this, the *shesheiya* artisans occupied the coveted stalls in the souk that were closest to the mosque.

Nana's generation, growing up in the 1920's and 30's, had witnessed the effects of colonization by the French and the introduction of European habits, foods, and codes of dress, often to the detriment of Tunisian cultural traditions. By the late 1950's when Tunisia regained its independence, the market for *shesheiya* had all but disappeared, selling more to the tourists than to Tunisians themselves. In Nana's family, the craft, the business, and the family's source of wealth had died with her father.

On our promenade, Aicha and I pass the house of Fatima Bouseha, a famous Tunisian singer in the traditional *mizouit* style. She is proud of her origins in the medina, and choosing to keep her home there has been an important part of her popularity. A few steps later, we pass the alley my husband has pointed to many times: "This was where we lived." We have nothing but time, Aicha and I, and we decide to go take a look at the old family house. I had never noticed the name of the alley before: *Impasse des Tunisiens*. We walk about two thirds of the way in. On the left-hand side, occupying the last third of the alley, is the house, number 4. Its entrance has been permanently sealed with concrete. The stone walls look ancient and seem to sway and bend with their own age.

It has not been lived in for many years, this house. No one knows what happened to the present owner or where he can be reached. There had been rumors of his intentions to demolish Nana's house, purchase the house next door and build a much larger apartment complex. But Tunis, and the *medina* especially, has landmark preservation laws that are strictly enforced. Permits were not granted, and the building project was abandoned. Apparently, before he disappeared, he stripped the house of its antique tiles, every one, and sold them to a private buyer, probably European.

Nana's house stands empty, and I wish with all my heart that we could break in, explore, revive the structure and atmosphere—and the spaciousness-- that the entire family associates with the place. Her children mark the moment when Nana sold her house as the beginning of her decline in health. She was diagnosed with diabetes soon after and gradually lost much of the strength for which she had been known. Discord sprouted between the siblings, some of whom felt others were to blame for influencing her move. Shortly before she died, she made her children promise that one of them would build another house and unite the family under one roof again.

As we stand in front of the abandoned home, we look up at the now gargantuan fig tree that has its roots somewhere in the courtyard. Its uppermost branches dwarf the building, and its large fleshy leaves hover over the walls protectively, like dark green open hands. It has deposited hundreds of ripe figs on the cobblestone walkway. The blood red droppings litter the alley, and we can see great quantities of green figs still clinging to the upper branches, inaccessible. Traditionally, the removal of a fig tree or an olive tree brings bad luck. Latifa tells of a neighbor who chopped down a fig tree in her yard and subsequently lost three members of the family to freak accidents and unexplained illness. This one definitely has the aspect of a sentinel, and I wonder what its fate will be.

An old woman opens her door behind us. Her face is deeply wrinkled, she has several teeth missing, and I'm quite sure she's been observing us all this time. She asks us in Arabic who we are looking for. I try to answer that we are from the Naouai family, that I am the wife of Allala Naouai, who lived here as a child. I have mangled it, and she takes my hand and directs us back out to the *rue de la Riviere*, pointing to number 20 where the Naouai family has lived for many years. I thank her and pretend we are heading that way before turning around again to continue our journey to Mouldi's shop.

BISMILLAH

Imagine this. No step or undertaking, small or large, is attempted without first saying *bismillah*, in the Name of God. You say *bismillah* as you step into a car, when you take a drink of water, before you eat a meal (especially at someone else's house, or at a restaurant, or if you try something you've never tasted before), before you attempt something about which you are unsure. *Bismillah* before anything you do for the first time, anything involving risk. Latifa says it before she lowers the fish into the boiling oil or sticks the sharp kitchen knife into the tight skin of the huge watermelon. You say *bismillah* as a blessing upon crossing the threshold of a new home, as an appeal for protection when reaching into a dark corner, upon beginning an exam or when entering the hospital. The butcher says it before he slaughters the lamb. In fact, as you sit up in bed and turn from your pillow in the morning, as you lower your feet to the floor, before you take the first steps of each and every day, you whisper *bismillah*. Simple as a breath.

CORNER STORE

On a scrappy, exposed street corner in the Bardo neighborhood where Latifa lives, sits a small fruit and vegetable stand where we pick up last-minute items for dinner. It is run by a slight and sun-wrinkled man who, in New York City, would certainly be mistaken for a homeless person. He looks about 70 years old. Most of his teeth are missing, and those remaining are stained a dark brown. He is dressed in rags; a pair of calf-length pants, smudged and worn, and a frayed, sleeveless t-shirt, once red, with a faded image of Hawaii on the front. He is barefoot and wears, on his cleanshaven head, the white *aracheiya*, a crocheted skull cap worn by many Muslim men, much like the Jewish *yarmulke*, but larger. His skin is tanned a dark, burnished brown and the white stubble of his beard appears to be at least three days old. Except for his feet, he appears clean, and he gives off no odor. He greets us graciously as we approach, '*Aslemma*'.

He works his life's requirements around his trade. As we approach, he is sitting outside on a low stool, grilling plum tomatoes for his dinner, on the *canoun* in front of him on the ground.

The small, terracotta stove is shaped like a bowl and contains a handful of glowing coals, just enough to cook a meal or send up a curl of incense smoke. On the shady side of the sidewalk, a mattress made of two sleeping bags, folded onto cardboard, and a once cheerfully-colored pillow serve as his bed. I have seen him sleeping there during siesta time, as soundly at ease as if he were on a daybed in a private home. His customers know not to disturb him while he rests. His *canoun*, as well as a bucket of water and a sharp knife, allow him to prepare meals of grilled vegetables and toasted bread, perhaps even the occasional fish or lamb chop, though every time I've seen him cook, he is roasting tomatoes.

In the back of his store and to the left, just past the peppers and hidden by a door covered by the poster of a monkey eating a banana, is his bathroom, comprising a toilet and hand sink. His store is barely three meters squared, and like most such produce stands, is open to the street. He sells modest quantities of whatever is in season, which he purchases wholesale from the market and brings back to the store in a turquoise-blue painted hand truck. These days, at the peak of summer, he sells tomatoes, peppers, onions, and potatoes inside. The waist-high shallow bins have been covered with oilcloth bearing a motif of once purple grapes. The cloth is ripped in places, revealing the hand-made wooden bins beneath, worn with age but sturdy still. A bare bulb hangs at the end of a serpentine wire from the ceiling. He turns it on only at night.

Outside, on one side of the door, under an awning, he has watermelons and honeydew melons piled directly onto the ground. On the other side, more bins contain figs, peaches, grapes and the tiny yellow *bougidma* pears. These perishable summer fruits are protected from the sun by a shade of remarkable invention; a kind of patchwork quilt made from scrap rectangles of tarp, oil cloth, burlap bags, even pressboard and plastic Coca-Cola signs written in Arabic. These various pieces have been sewn together with nylon string, twine, odd lengths of brightly colored electrical wire, shoelaces, even a bent up and reshaped clothes hanger. In the daytime, the sun illuminates the various colors and textures, creating a beautiful stained-glass window of recycled goods. The effect reminds me of a bird's nest I see in NYC every spring above the awning of a pizzeria, cobbled together from grasses and yarn, dog hair and the occasional sparkle of Christmas tree tinsel.

The vendor interrupts his peeling of the tomatoes he has just grilled and smiles generously at us. We are knocking on some watermelons to choose the right one. He neither helps us nor offers advice, as we seem to know what we want. He seems affable and not in the least resentful of the interruption to his dinner preparations. Customers will come and go, he seems to say, they will either buy something or they won't, and the tomatoes will be there, waiting for him in the *canoun*, whose embers glow orange in the fading light.

OULA

We begin early in the morning. 6 AM is best, before the sun is hot and high.

We select the workplace for its exposure to the sun and protection from the wind, usually an interior courtyard. We wash the tiled courtyard floor with buckets of clear water, scrubbing with the brush and rinsing away the dust. This is where the *couscous* will be prepared and dried. We hang clean drapes over the open banisters as a barrier against the dust.

Quiet anticipation builds as we prepare coffee, music, incense, and gather the utensils we will need: several large bowls, at least five kilos of semolina, a large pot of salted water, a *couscousière*, and three different grades of *couscous* sieves-- *khamah*, for the first step of separating the semolina, *seneh* for the second step and to make the couscous fine, and *toleah* for the everyday medium grade couscous.

The *oula* arrives, and now the work can begin. She is traditionally a household helper, hired seasonally with the specific purpose of preparing the pantry essentials for autumn and winter. She is skilled in the preparation of drying and grinding spices, canning and pickling, and particularly in the preparation of *couscous*.

In the old days, my sisters tell me, there were usually enough daughters in any given household and enough knowledge, passed from one generation to the next, that the work could be done by the family without outside help. An entire day, or a weekend, would be devoted to preparing the pantry for a full year. Once the daughters were grown and had their own families, the quantities increased, and the spoils were divided. The entire event had the aspect of celebration and abundance, and it served as an absolute declaration of the home as the domain of the woman.

As women in Tunisian cities of the 1980's and 90's entered universities and then the workforce, additional labor was recruited from the country where most people still lived according to tradition. Hence, the rise in popularity of the *oula*. Nowadays, anyone who wants to eat authentically Tunisian food needs the help of an *oula* to make it happen. The alternative is to buy packaged *couscous* from the grocery store, and the comparison is the same as packaged to fresh pasta. The taste and texture are worlds apart.

The *oula* arrives and seems to come from a very different world. She enters the garden, wrapped in a traditional ivory-hued *sefseri* which billows gently as she walks. Her gaze, when it meets mine, is not subdued but direct and full of calm curiosity. Her skin is a shade darker than her city compatriots and has more vitality. She's missing a few teeth, but the ones that remain are a brilliant white and look strong. Her body, too, looks strong and alive, despite her sixty plus years. Her hands, like her feet when she removes her *shlekas*, are clean and broad. Underneath the *sefseri* she wears a flowered skirt, a t-shirt, and a brightly patterned head scarf, wrapped neatly around the head and tucked behind the ears. She wears gold earrings and a simple gold bangle, but no wedding ring. I ask her about an unusual tattoo on her right wrist, what looks like a geometric tribal design about two inches long and half that width, in a blueish-green hue. I have seen similar tattoos on the cheeks of older women whose ancestors came from desert tribes, the Berbers. She explains that she broke that arm when she was a girl. After the bones healed, the family gave her the tattoo for its protective powers.

We have laid out a workspace at one end of the now pristine courtyard, including layers of carpets, blankets, and sheets, as well as pillows on which to sit comfortably. We sit facing each other, one leg tucked in and the other stretched out. We pour our coffee, put on the radio, and begin to work. Every now and then, sister Latifa interrupts her chores to check in or lend a hand.

Here is how you make *couscous*:

Pour a workable quantity of semolina, about 4 cups, into the largest bowl. Add salted water to evenly dampen the semolina, maybe 1/4 cup.

Mix with clean hands.

Pass the semolina through the *khamah* into another bowl, by swishing the sieve in a circular motion.

Shake the bowl gently back and forth to even out the contents .

Now pass the couscous through the *seneh* into a third bowl, in the same way you did using the *khamah*. This final bowl is placed on an incline,with the finished *couscous* always toward the back so that the batch you are working on is closest to you.

Gently shake the final product in the large bowl to ensure even distribution.

The final step is to pass all of the finished couscous through the *toleah* to work out any larger clumps.

Moisten the entire quantity of finished *couscous* with a little bit of olive oil. Hand mix gently until it is evenly distributed.

Put water in the bottom half of a *couscousière*, add five cloves to prevent mold.

Treat the top half of the *couscousière* with a light coating of olive oil.

Wet a strip of cloth and tie it around the seam between the two halves.

Fill the top half halfway with the freshly made *couscous*. When you see the steam rise, remove the *couscous* grains. It will have doubled in volume.

Dump the *couscous* onto a clean sheet or *sefseri*, break it up so no lumps form, and cover it with a clean cloth. Add consecutive batches of steamed *couscous* until all of it has been processed.

Pass the steamed *couscous* once more through the *khamah* to separate the grains.

Spread all the *couscous* out onto a sheet (straw mat, wool blanket, sheets layered one atop the other). Let dry in the sun for 3-4 days, collecting it and bringing it inside at night to protect against dew. A few times a day, the *couscous* should be redistributed gently, on hands and knees, with broad, slow sweeps of the open hand, to ensure equal exposure to air and sun. When it is completely dry, your supply of *couscous* is ready to be stored and parceled out, as needed.

"*Khit alik!*" You've crossed the line! My husband's cousin, Lyes, interrupts us at the door. He drops a box of nut pastries at our feet and enters the house. Sister Latifa explains to me that traditionally, men are not allowed into the house during the *oula* because the making of the *couscous* is an occasion for women to get together and gossip and celebrate, let their hair loose. If a man breaks the circle, he is obliged to bring a gift of seasonal fruits or sweets for the women to share.

TO MARKET

Our house is located at Soliman Plage. The town of Soliman is about two kilometers away, too far to walk to in the morning sun, and our family is too big for us to carry the groceries on a bicycle. We go to market every two or three days, and supplement with bread and milk from the nearby general store. Today is very windy. The black flag is up at the beach and we see a grandmother hurrying home with a small child in her arms, wrapped up in a brightly colored scarf against the elements. The wind whips about, distributing fine yellow sand, as light as powdered sugar.

We walk to the square to catch a ride into town. It is empty this time of day, though the garbage bins are testimony to the crowds that gathered here last night; paper ice cream cups spill out over the top, and pizza crusts, and the greasy newsprint squares used to serve *bambalone*, a kind of fried dough dipped in sugar. The taxicabs are waiting. Each will take four passengers into town for five hundred *millimes* each, about fifty cents per person.

We embark with two men, one of whom has decided to

abandon his day of fishing because of the wind. His equipment is behind us, in the trunk, and the dismantled pole juts out just beside my head. Everyone is silent during the ride. The howling of the wind is constant, the sand and dust swirl dramatically on the road ahead, and plastic bags and debris can be seen whipping through the sky. We pass a flock of sheep grazing in large, tree-less fields. We arrive in town, and clamber awkwardly out of the small car. We take a breath, square our shoulders. We are never early enough to beat the heat, even though now it is only nine in the morning. The *coffa*, or market basket, will be heavy soon and we are still half-asleep. We stop in our favorite cafe, and a nod from our waiter brings two steaming *capucins* and a bottle of Safia mineral water.

As we walk up the street, a barber scoops water from a bucket using a cut-off plastic water bottle. He splashes it onto the street and sidewalk in front of his business, anchoring the dust that oth-erwise comes in through the open door. He will repeat this ritual several times throughout the day. Everything is quiet, an echo of our sleepy state, and then we turn the corner and suddenly the street bursts into life: a cacophony of colors and sounds, activity and purpose, conveys a sense of abundance and invitation that quickens our step.

Women, dressed in brightly patterned dresses and head-scarves, or draped in diaphanous, white *sefseris*, clutch their market baskets, or the hands of young children, purses clenched in their teeth or tucked away in their bosoms. They look regal and festive and they carry themselves with a sense of unques-tionable authority that captures my imagination. They survey the goods and make the rounds before deciding where and what to purchase.

Some of the merchants are still setting up their stands while others cry out their wares or greet each other in a surge of morning energy. Hand trucks are everywhere, dented and battered. Essentially big, metal cribs to which two bicycle wheels have been affixed, they are pulled or pushed like a wheelbarrow with only one handle. At the end of the day, empty, they get hooked up to a bicycle or donkey and carted home. They have been painted dozens of times, and the layers of different blues are visible where the paint has chipped. Some have enormous tuna fish tails tied to them for good luck as they carry loads of parsley or crates of tomatoes. They deftly maneuver through impossibly narrow aisles made by the vendors who sell just outside the market hall. These are mostly younger men in their twenties, wearing base-ball hats and worn t-shirts with American slogans. The older vendors look like they might have had a run of bad luck, or are starting over. They have no official claim to the space they occu-py and they are working against time; the effects of the sun will soon destroy their merchandise if it is not sold. Some have beach umbrellas to protect them and their wares, but many are selling directly from wheelbarrows or crates. The prices are lower here, the fruits slightly smaller or with a tinge of age, a few bruises, artfully hidden. A peach vendor unstacks his crates and dusts off the peaches row by row, in an almost meditative rhythm. He uses a rudimentary hand broom made from loose straws that are bound to an unfinished dowel with a piece of black rubber. He finishes one crate and arranges the peaches in neat, attractive pyramids.

I notice again how small many of the fruits and vegetables are, compared to their American counterparts. The flavors are much stronger, as if concentrated, and I wonder if the intensity of the sun and the lack of water are contributing factors. Every-thing available at the market is indigenous to Tunisia, except the bananas, so everything is local and in season.

It is high summer here, and nearing the end of peach season.

There are conventional peaches the size of my fist with dark, yellow-orange flesh. They are sweet and tangy and dripping with juice and they are my favorites. Tunisia is also where I was introduced to the flat, donut peaches, with their aromatic, white meat, long before they ever appeared at Fairway. Figs are available, too, pale green, and the larger, black figs, both split and showing the deep red of their insides.

Everything is methodically stacked, with a speed and lightness of touch that seems in contradiction with the strong, calloused hands of the vendors. There are melons of various shapes and sizes, most resembling honeydew or cantaloupe or crenshaw. These can be found on the roadside, too, sold directly from trucks, along with watermelon, *deleah*, a summertime staple. The season has begun for grapes, black or green, and the only seedless grapes are the tiny, green vintners' rejects, which are also the least expensive. When a vendor sees me eyeing the fruit, he clips off a small bunch and gives it to me, and the cool grapes are sweet and crisp, the grapes of my childhood memories. Pears, too, and new apples are in season. We buy one kilo of small apples of the palest green, some with a rosy blush, and I know they will be slightly tart, with a nice crunch to them. We also buy one kilo of tiny yellow pears, the size of my thumb, our children's favorite. They are aptly named *bougidma*, which means little bite.

We pass by a ten-year-old boy selling yellow *hindi*, cactus pears, from a large *harissa* can. He must have picked them this morning to sell at market. His dusty, blue bicycle leans against the wall behind him. With a tweezer, he deftly pulls the cactus spines from his fingers. We will buy them later, at the end of the summer, when the meat inside turns from pale yellow to bright fuchsia. All the while, the vendors are calling out their wares, the prices, the qualities that will make them irresistible. The cries are loud and sharp, and belie a fierce competition; a joyous concert that reminds me of the sound of migrating geese.

We turn into the covered market hall. We are out of the sun and it takes a moment for our eyes to adjust. The air is cool. Waiters from the nearby café glide through, trays held in front of them or overhead. They carry the morning orders of the merchants; small glasses of coffee or tea, and a tall bottle of mineral water, already sweating. Another waiter walks behind, deftly carrying a lit *houka*. The sweet-smelling smoke curls up above us.

The market space is constructed from concrete pillars that support a vaulted, exposed brick ceiling. Electrical lines cross like spider webs from pillar to pillar, each stall lit by a bare bulb which dangles from a cord. There are only two walls and the air circulates agreeably. The stalls are neatly arranged. Each vendor delineates his space with stacks of plastic crates; yellow, blue, red, green, all bleached pale with the dust and grime of ages.

Most of the vegetables are here inside, protected from the heat. The produce is less carefully arranged. There are mounds of tomatoes, curvy, thin cucumbers with a tough, almost furry skin, bunches of parsley and spinach, big, dark green pumpkins called *kraa*, and the sections that have been cut from them, bright orange, seeds hanging. Peppers are another staple during the summer: *halou* (sweet), *miski* (medium), and *haar* (hot). They are all relatively small and an even, emerald green color. Although the hot peppers seem to be somewhat longer and thinner than the others, with a slightly puckered skin, the only way to tell for sure is to nick the skin and daringly touch it with the tip of your tongue.

The vendors inside are older, many wearing the traditional white, crocheted cap, the *arrakheia*, and a faded blue merchant's jacket cut like a doctor's lab coat. These men have earned their places in the market, they have paid for their spots and the prices are comparatively higher. The vendors do not cry out as loudly, unless they have added something to their wares. The quality advertises itself. There is an air of resignation, of mild disdain for the customers. We sometimes have trouble with money here, when the vendors 'forget' to give us part of our change, or where slight of hand provides us with unasked for merchandise.

Everything is sold by the pound, except for bunches of greens or the smaller melons. The scales are ancient; two bent and rusted pans suspended over a heavy, iron base, and four weights: 250g, 500g, one kilo and 2 kilos. The selected goods are deftly scooped into the pans which have been made from tomato sauce cans that have been split open and soldered together, much the way we used to make skirts from a pair of old jeans. Customers are discouraged from selecting their own produce here, but some of the housewives manage to throw in a few choice pieces. This breach would not be as readily tolerated from a male customer, but most of the customers are women, the keepers of the kitchen. Occasionally there is an older, distinguished looking man, a bachelor, perhaps, or someone temporarily abandoned by his family gone ahead on vacation. We request two kilos of white onions and they are added until the scale tips. The sturdier vegetables go directly into the shopping basket, which we hold open to receive our bounty.

We still need meat for *couscous* and fresh mint, which we save for last to keep it from wilting. At the meat counter, the butcher is already sweating. He wipes dead flies from the refrigerated display case and arranges veal on a plastic tray, which he props with an old two-by-four for better viewing. The butcher's block is enormous, the quintessential surface for chopping through bone and gristle. It is a section of tree trunk, stripped of its bark, about two feet thick and two feet in diameter. This is attached to three smaller tree trunks, which serve as the legs.

The cleaver comes down with a disconcerting whack as the

customer, a man, argues with the butcher about the amount of fat on the pieces he is cutting for his order. Once the meat is wrapped in thick, gray paper, the butcher makes him wait to pay, ostensibly busy with another order. On the floor, a blue plastic bucket, the same as we use for our washing, contains intestines of all kinds, shiny and gray and convoluted, just the way they look in anatomy books.

On a stainless steel table, goats' heads, one with its tongue hanging out, drip blood onto the floor. The feet of the goats are in a pile nearby, the hair matted, flies buzzing about. Skinned lambs, headless and footless, hang from hooks above the display case, alongside the head of a cow, intact with a soft, tawny muzzle, eyes closed. I wonder how my family and friends back home would react to such stark and damning evidence of the carnivorous appetite. Our benign and plastic-wrapped packages at Shoprite bear little resemblance. I find myself considering the benefits of vegetarianism.

Despite the abundance of meat, the orders are small. Even with our family of fifteen (not counting the visitors that may or may not pop in around dinnertime) we only purchase one kilo of lamb, half of which will go in the freezer. Meat is expensive and most people can afford just enough to season their food. In any case, Tunisian cuisine, I have learned, relies on the art of creating abundance out of very little, and the most important ingredient is the atmosphere of the meal, the gesture of generosity. The *couscous*, shared between us, will taste even more delicious for having just enough meat.

We pass the fish section. Beautiful hand painted murals with leaping tuna, swordfish, even dolphins, frolic among rolling waves and disproportionately small ships. The tiled counters are almost bare; here and there, small piles of *rougets* or sardines or eel, spread out a bit to look like more and arranged on a bed of seaweed. The selection is decidedly sparse compared to the fish market in Tunis, where everything is neatly stacked and there is a greater variety of seafood. Most of the choicest fish, unfortunately, get shipped to Italy, resulting in deplorably high prices for the Tunisian consumer.

As we leave the covered market, we pass the vendors who sit in the thresholds; older men, selling bunches of fresh mint or bay leaves or verbena. They sit on overturned plastic buckets, their wares emitting the most delicious perfumes as they wave them in the air and shake them to release their aromas. We buy two bunches of mint and one of verbena from a deeply wrinkled and sun-browned man of about seventy who smiles brightly at us despite several missing teeth as he wishes us a good day.

On the way to the taxi stand we buy bread from the bakery; essentially a room with an oven and stainless steel racks of bread and a simple counter to sell them from. We buy three *baguettes* and one large, round *tabouna*, the traditional Tunisian bread. As we step into the taxi, we break off a piece of the warm bread for the ride. Home again, home again, jiggety-jig.

RAMADAN

We arrive in Tunis at L'Aeroport de Carthage just after noon, the sun high and white, at its zenith. After the jumble of passport control, baggage claim, missing suitcases, we stop at duty-free for beer and wine before we exit to a cluster of weary relatives and friends awaiting their travelers. It is the holy month of *Ramadan* here in Tunisia. As in the Muslim world everywhere, people are fasting from sun-up to sun-down, their lives determined and drastically altered by the phases of the moon and the minutes of the clock. Three weeks of *Ramadan* have passed, and so one week remains until *Eïd*, the celebration which marks the culmination and closure of *Ramadan* and return to normal life. For three days now, the weather has been hot; Tunisian hot, 110 degrees in the shade. *Ramadan* dictates, as my brother-in-law explains, 'no eat, no drink, no look at the woman', from dawn until dusk. These long summer days test both the will and the spirit. The old, the infirm, nursing mothers, and children are exempt because of the arduous nature of the injunction. This is also a time of prayer, of contemplation, of empathy with the poor, of altruism and forgiveness. Because the Muslim calendar follows the lunar cycles, *Ramadan* falls 10 days earlier each year than the year before, so that, for example, *Ramadan* in winter offers a completely different experience from *Ramadan* during the summer: different hours, different recipes, different atmosphere.

Now, as we navigate slow-moving traffic on the way to our home, the streets are empty, stores shuttered. Later, around 4 PM, chickens will be slowly spinning on rotisseries, filling the air with their heavenly aroma and testing the piety of those nearby. Bakers will pile their steaming baguettes into baskets, and the melon sellers will unhook the backs of their pickup trucks and put out their scales: 250 millimes/kilo. But for now, the towns are markedly deserted, save for one creature, nearly overlooked. In front of a dark storefront that advertises fresh, grilled meats, *mischoui*, a young, white camel with a tufted hump, fore and hind legs immaculately folded beneath him, sits in the crisscrossed shadows of an electric tower, completely immobile. I wonder if it isn't a statue and then, just before we pass, I catch one slow, heavy-lidded blink.

At 6 PM, people will begin spilling out of their homes and stumble onto to the beach, unable to resist the call of the water. Minutes before the sun drops behind the horizon, they will drink in the wet of the sea through their weary pores, mouths parched, bellies hollow, and feel refreshed, remember gratitude. Others will scurry to market to purchase last minute items for the breakfast that comes with sunset, each day a few minutes earlier: 8:46; 8:44; 8:42. Every Muslim has a calendar with the exact times of sunrise and sunset for each day of Ramadan. The younger generations print them from the internet for their elders to display on the fridge then download an app for themselves. They have been weaned into the spiritual practice from the age of nine or ten, first abstaining until noon, then, by the time they are in high school, fasting in tandem with their parents. Even when Muslims immigrate to other countries where they are the minority, many continue this practice, one of the five pillars of Islam.

Initially, I found this idea of sacrifice almost inconceivable. I had gone five hours, seven hours maybe, without food, but never an entire day, let alone thirty. I think of myself as having compassion for those in need, but I have never actually been tested by recreating the circumstances of hunger and thirst. On the other hand, there is the call to spirit that beckons, with its promise of connection and transcendence. Many spiritual traditions, I know, include fasting as a means of opening the heart and connecting with source. As the body becomes accustomed to deprivation over a prescribed number of days, the spirit derives nourishment from that empty space. It strengthens as it is liberated from the demands of the body, and takes flight. The 27th day of Ramadan marks the day when God spoke to Mohammed in the desert: "Write this down, what I am about to tell you," and the Holy Koran was born.

Ali had never really subscribed to the practice of Ramadan, eager to leave it behind with other elements of his native culture which he sometimes found burdensome or constricting. On September 11th, 2001, however, everything changed. For the first time, I saw him lose his composure. As he watched the repeated images on television of the airplanes hitting the towers, he broke down. The Muslims of his childhood could be temperamental, yes, even mean-spirited, but not capable of the irreparable violence we had witnessed on TV. Later, he would intensely analyze the politics of the chain of events that that led to the attack, but his first response was a need for a reparation of sorts, a need to tip the scales in favor of peace; to practice kindness, generosity, compassion, faith, and moderation.

So, *Ramadan* became an offering, and he still practices it

faithfully when his health allows. I admire and envy his fortitude. His life is otherwise devoted to the making and sharing of earthly pleasures - food, drink, romance, beauty, children. I observe him closely as he initially struggles against fatigue, resistance, hunger, thirst. After a few days, though, I witness a kind of melting away of all that might be extraneous or use up precious energy; contention, impatience, worry, agitation of whatever kind recede into the background as mere consciousness from moment to moment becomes the primary focus. The system conserves energy as it must, and as the days go by I find him to be more relaxed, peaceful, even contemplative, although he is also without question more tired and less productive.

Observing *Ramadan* is challenging for him as a business owner and, though I have expressed a desire to accompany him on his fasting journey, he has always asked me not to. He wants to spare me the struggle of deprivation and cites our cultural and educational differences, but he also knows he will rely on me more heavily during this time to keep things in order, to fill in more as he slows down, to remind him when he forgets. So, I keep my fasting to abstinence from alcohol and pork during the holy month of *Ramadan* and celebrate *Eïd* with a glass of wine.

One year I insisted on joining him and made it through the first day with far less duress than I'd expected. I felt somewhat irritated in the morning, the unsettling feeling of routine interrupted, caffeine withdrawal, and then, sometime around two o'clock in the afternoon, a sense of spaciousness settled over me—a feeling of having incredible stores of time and energy at my disposal. Ali kept checking in, expecting a breakdown, but I felt pretty stable for most of the day, except for debilitating attacks of thirst every now and then. At sundown, we broke our fast with water (oh, the beauty, the grace of it), and milky tea, dates, and plain cake. An hour or so later, a soup, then dinner quite late, around

11. Our stomachs had tightened and couldn't take more than a few bites of lighter foods: rice pilaf, steamed vegetables, slow-cooked stews. I felt good, proud of myself for having completed the day. Somewhere in the middle of the second day, however, Ali looked at me, like a sailor watching for storms, and said, "Eat something, please. You need to eat something". And that was it. Someday, I will try again, perhaps when *Ramadan* occurs during the winter, when the days are shorter and once the kids have left home. Once Ali and I are perhaps living in Tunisia, immersed in the rhythm of the lunar calendar, and the slower cadence of *Ramadan* outside the relentless pressures of NYC.

This summer, however, the kids and I have eaten just before relatives come in their cars to pick us up. We are invited to a wedding party that takes place late at night, after everyone has eaten. We will go to Nana's house and eat again with them as they break their fast, then drive to the party together. As we enter Tunis, we pass many cafés, open for business now, each table set with an array of foods, bread piled high, olives, jugs of water, everything ready to go. Men sit in groups around the table, hands folded politely in their laps, waiting for the minute hand to click to 8:42. *Saha schribtik!*

MARRIAGE

Great excitement! Ali's nephew and our children's favorite cousin is getting engaged. We have packed some elegant clothes for the event, selected chiffon outfits in pastel florals for the aunts. When we arrive in Tunisia, preparations are already underway. My husband's sister and the mother of the groom, is uncharacteristically nervous. I soon grasp that this is a big event, more like what we would consider to be a full-blown wedding.

While the party is the fiancées responsibility, the future groom and his family must appear with gifts. My sister-in-law and her daughter go out to purchase them. Our extended family gathers for dinner and to inspect and the goods and deem them worthy. The gifts are beautiful and make an effort to include both the traditional and the modern. A sumptuously silk-upholstered basket contains the traditional gifts: a set of elaborately embossed silver vanity items, all to be used in preparation for the bride's wedding night. There is a pair of elevated slippers for the hammam, a traditional fan, a candlestick to light the henna preparations, a plate and knife used to apply the henna, a pear-shaped flask containing khol for the eyes, an apple-shaped flask for face powder, and a perfume flask as well. A pair of lace embroidered mitts for the henna are included in this basket, and the moss-green henna powder itself. Traditionally, the family of the groom is responsible for the application of henna on the wedding night. The finer the henna and the more expert the application, the darker the henna appears on the skin of the hands and feet. And since dark henna ensures a long and harmonious marriage, it is seen as evidence of the mother-in-law's approval and support of the union.

The modern gift consists of a contemporary gold and diamond jewelry ensemble comprising a necklace, a bracelet and earrings, and, of course, a matching diamond engagement ring. No one can tell me why the flasks of the traditional set are in the shape of an apple and a pear. "It's always been that way", they say. And I realize that tradition is perhaps most faithfully upheld when it is neither questioned or analyzed.

Countdown to the engagement party. More preparations, phone calls to husbands – don't forget this or that, please pick up the other. My sister's tiny apartment is filled with dressing and fussing women. The groom's sister, for whom this event serves also as a kind of coming of age party, has gone, accompanied by our intrigued fifteen-year-old daughter to the hairdressers. They are absent for nearly eight hours. It is wedding season, after all. She returns transformed, dramatically coiffed with spirals of glittered hair snaking about her head and made up like a diva. No expense has been spared. Dresses, too expensive to purchase, are rented for the occasion, at prices the equivalent of a week's wages or more. Our youngest daughter, six years old, is terribly upset, disappointed with the elegant dress I purchased especially for the occasion. Compared with her younger cousin's extravagant pink and white satin, three-tiered affair, it looks too plain. She is despondent and I do my best to assure her that she, too, looks beautiful.

The gentlemen finally show up and there is some commotion. The father of the prospective groom and his family had expressed concern about the timing of the thing. The young man has one year to go to finish his university studies and they had urged him to wait. They have not yet arrived and there is fear that they may not show up in protest. The horror of this possibility is contemplated and both groom and mother are upset. Finally, they arrive and we all set off, about thirty of us, in five cars. We arrive at the bride's house, a big mansion in a much fancier part of town, and debark at the bottom of the driveway. En masse, as tradition dictates, the family of the groom moves as one, ululating and singing as we walk up the driveway, procession style. The bride's extended family and friends are already sitting at tables, of which there must be twenty or more. The fiancée is in full regalia and sits on an upholstered silk throne, immobile and looking somewhat frightened. Flanking her are her mother, her father, her grandmother and an aunt. To the side, a traditional *mizuit* band begins to play as we approach. There is a moment of discomfort as both families realize how different they are from each other. There are differences in lifestyle, in education, in socio-economic status. This is a modern marriage, two young people who met at university, who share ideas and preferences and friends. The families were almost an afterthought in their union and yet, now, the weight and significance of their presence and participation becomes clear. Once the introductions begin, however, accompanied by the obligatory profusion of kisses, the apprehensions fade and are quickly replaced by the Tunisian propensity for celebration.

Both extended families are seated at tables in the expansive, lavish garden, and trays of goodies are brought around without interruption: *baklava*, sweet strawberry smoothies or home-made lemonade, ice cream in paper cups, savory pastries, filled with mushroom and cheese or egg and tuna, almond sweets, flavored with orange water. During this time, people come up and dance, usually by family group, first the immediate family of the finacée, then that of the future groom, then the parents of both, then groups of cousins from one side, then from the other, then the aunts all together, then the uncles, etc. The children run about ecstatically, chasing each other, discovering a family of cats, threatening to knock over the five-tiered cake that has just been brought in perched precariously on a very ornate stand and beginning to melt in the sultry evening.

At one point the gifts from our nephew's family to his fiancée are brought out and displayed. The jewelry is ceremoniously put on the fiancée by my sister, whose fingers fumble at the enormity of the task. Finally, the young man slips the ring on his lady's finger, amidst much ululating and flashing of cameras. Our dear nephew, pale with fright at the beginning of the evening, now looks quite relaxed and content. As we bump into each other in sweaty groups, dancing to his happiness, I am moved to tears. When I first met him, he was ten years old, the age of my oldest son now.

Later, I ask about the actual wedding. Why the extravagance of the engagement party? And how can the wedding compete? The engagement legitimizes their dating, I am informed, allows them to go out unchaperoned. And the wedding? Just wait! That will be something to remember. An extended feast of fifteen days will include a week during which all unmarried female relatives and friends of the bride come to her house to help her prepare her trousseau. Sheets and towels, drapes and rugs, will be cleaned, ironed, packed for departure to her new home. Plates and cups and pots and pans will all be washed and dried and stacked.

Any personal items, clothing, books, pictures, will be mended, cleaned, wrapped up. All of her possessions will be gathered together for viewing before they are moved on the day of her wedding celebration. In a twenty-five-year-old picture of another sister-in-law, she presides, smiling, over an entire courtyard filled with brimming, handled baskets ready to be transported.

The bride will be taken to the hammam and scrubbed, washed and waxed. Her eyebrows will be shaped and every bit of body hair removed save the long, luxurious hair on her head. Henna will be applied to the hair, and once again to the hands and feet, over the course of three days, just prior to the wedding. The bride will avoid touching water in order to preserve the darkness and clarity of the henna designs.

All of this will be accompanied by much visiting, ululating, chatting, weeping, arguing, cooking, eating, reminiscing and celebration. On the wedding day itself, the bride will wear another rented dress, sometimes two different ones if the party is a long one, and these dresses are like rhinestone studded battleships, with jutting shoulders and wide, ankle length skirts, the entire affair sparkling with intricately patterned stones. Another double throne in white satin will be delivered for her to sit on and entertain from while her husband makes the rounds on the floor.

Separate celebrations for the bride's family and for the groom's friends will be organized, with much cheering and joking in both camps, more music, more sweets. More celebrations, at least two, for the signing of the contract, and then the big party, the official wedding celebration with both families and countless friends. Finally, the two will leave as one from the bride's childhood home, trousseau in tow, and their life as a couple will begin. Children will follow close upon the wedding, hopefully within the first year, *Inch'allah*!

CIRCUMCISION

When our second son was born, we decided to have him circumcised in Tunisia, with a traditional celebration. Our firstborn had been circumcised hours after his birth in the hospital at my mother-in-law's suggestion. She had believed that the process would be more hygienic in the US. In her day, the man who circumcised boys was the *tahar,* the neighborhood barber, also schooled in the art of bloodletting for people suffering from an excess of passion or heat. I think she was also making a concession to me. Knowing that I was not Muslim, she thought I might have objections to doing it in Tunisia. She was a woman of great understanding and generosity of spirit.

A boy's circumcision is a very important celebration, particularly for the mother of the father, and Ali was the first of her sons to have a son. So, when a second boy was born, we decided to have the circumcision in Tunisia. This would be the culmination of her life as a mother. We had assured ourselves of the modernity of the clinics where the circumcisions were performed, and felt no misgivings about the procedure. My son would be barely a year old.

Typically, boys in Tunisia are circumcised between the ages of one and six. The ceremony begins with a big parade, during which the boy is led to the knife in a horse-drawn cart, traditionally dressed in gold-embroidered pants and vest, golden slippers and a red felt *shesheiya*. A garland of jasmine blossoms hangs from his neck. He sits on the driver's box, terrified, sandwiched between his mother and father. The cart advances slowly, accompanied by a band playing traditional music, boisterous and slightly discordant. Ululating women march alongside the cart, children run about, and neighbors stand outside their doors, following the parade with knowing eyes. Once the circumcision has taken place, family and friends gather to celebrate, dancing and eating far into the night.

While we had opted out of the horse-drawn cart, thinking it might send our baby screaming in fright, we began preparations for the party a week in advance. It would take place at my sister-in-law's house, because she had the biggest courtyard. We set to work finding a *mizouit* band and sent out invitations in typical Tunisian fashion, through the grapevine. A permit had to be acquired from the neighborhood municipal office for the party because of the live music.

The women set to the task of preparing the food days in advance. We procured every washing bucket from four different households. An extra refrigerator was hauled in. Two days before the party, the sisters started peeling and cutting and cooking in shifts. Great quantities of lamb stew with artichoke hearts and peas, *couscous osben* for fifty, little fried phyllo dough rolls called *sweba fatima*, and baked egg *tagine* with chicken and spinach cut into squares. The kitchen was packed with women stirring and tasting, talking and rushing in from the market with little bags of salt or another bunch of fresh mint. Nana presided over it all, sitting in a chair square in the middle of the kitchen, her watchful eyes missing nothing.

As the day of the circumcision approached, I started feeling anxious about the operation, worried for my son and the pain he might suffer, the possibility of infection in the merciless heat. I would come into the kitchen to warm a bottle of milk or to rinse out a glass, and Nana would catch my hand, look steadily into my eyes, and pat my arm reassuringly. We shared no common language but, as on many occasions before and since, we understood each other completely and I felt my fears diminish. In Tunisia, the event of the circumcision allows for a deep connection between the mother of the child and the father's mother, though it doesn't always pan out that way. The mother-in-law initiates her son's wife into the first of many fears in bringing a son into the world. Ideally, she becomes a source of support and comfort for the young mother, so that she in turn can be the same for her own son. On the night before the circumcision, I sat with Khalil sleeping in my arms, while my sisters-in-law applied the henna to my hands and feet and to his, just as tradition commands. During this hours-long process the family sang traditional songs, voices raspy, eyes glowing in the firelight of the *canoun*. The songs invoked the mercy of the *tahar* and described the worry and love a mother has for her child.

The following morning, with Khalil looking amazed by his newly painted feet, we traipsed off to the clinic. I fought the urge to grab him and run in the opposite direction. An hour later we emerged and brought him home to recover from the anesthesia. He spent the entire evening standing in the middle of the festivities with nothing on but an undershirt, taking everything in. He didn't seem to notice that something pretty dramatic had taken place. He didn't seem to be in pain. Still, I held him in my arms for most of the night. While friends and relatives came and ate and danced and tucked money into my hand or under Khalil's hat - the only part of the special outfit he would wear - Nana's gaze was on us, watchful and protective.

Mizouit carries a powerful beat, mesmerizing and wholly African. The drummers beat their *darbouka* with such fervor that many tape their fingers to avoid splitting them open. Occasionally during the dancing, one of the grownups would go into a trance and had to be carried off into a room to be revived. Everyone stepped in to help with what appeared to be a familiar occurrence.

At about 4 AM, the police showed up. They had come for the musicians, whose trail they had followed to my sister-in-law's house. Apparently, they had been stopped on the way to our gig and had evaded arrest for driving drunk without a valid license. While the police were explaining all of this to Ali and his sister, the musicians managed to scale the garden wall and escape. It was an entertaining end to a wonderful evening, and they were never heard from again, even though we had paid them only half their fee.

The following day we left for Monastir, a beach town just a few hours south. There we rented a hotel room and bathed Khalil's wound in the Mediterranean for a week, the accepted prescription for rapid healing from a circumcision. Indeed, he was not alone. The beach was dotted with naked little boys jumping around in the surf, their ordeal already a distant memory.

Circumcision Song
Translation from the Arabic to French by Yosra Nouai

Circoncisez oh circonciseur
Que Dieu vous donne la force et la santé
Ne faites pas mal à mon fils pour que je ne vous tienne pas rancune

Circumcise, oh circumcisor!
May God give you strength and health
Don't hurt my son or I will resent you

*Etant jeune tu seras un circoncis pour devenir tel un Chevalier sur sa
monture bien distinguer d'entre les jeunes hommes*

As a child you will be circumcised so that you may become a knight
on his mount, distinguished among young men

(refrain)

La **mère** du circoncis ou se trouve t- *elle ? sur mezzanine.* ! pour que je
la *felicite. Que Dieu préserve sa joie.*

The mother of the circumcised, where is she? On the mezzanine! So
that I may congratulate her. May God preserve her joy.

(refrain)

*Circoncisez oh circonciseur
Circoncisez-le , ne lui faites pas de mal
ses larmes coulent à flot* à cause de l'aiguisage de la lame

Circumcise, oh circumcisor!
Circumcise him, don't hurt him
His tears overflow as he hears the sharpening of the blade

(refrain)

Circoncisez mon fiston sur les bord du lit, n'ayez pas peur circonciseur

Circumcise my son on the edge of the bed, have no fear, circumcisor

(refrain)
Je lui ai fait la circoncision ça y est. je lui ai appris le coran et si Dieu

me donnait une longue vie, le jour de ses noces je lui amènerais sa femme à ses côtés.

I had him circumcised, it's all done. I taught him the Koran and, if God gives me a long life, on the day of his wedding I'll escort his wife to his side.

(refrain)

Etant jeune, tu seras un circoncis pour devenir plus tard un jeune marié bien distinguer des autres jeunes montant une monture bien imposante

As a child, you will be circumcised so that you may someday become a young bridegroom, distinguished among other youths, astride an impressive mount.

Circoncisez oh circonciseur
Que Dieu vous donne la force et la santé
Ne faites pas mal à mon fils pour que je ne vous tienne pas rancune

Circumcise, oh circumcisor!
May God give you strength and health
Don't hurt my son or I will resent you.

SUPERSTITION

When our children were babies, and most deliciously adorable, Ali was forever begging me not to wash them. We would come back from the park and I would herd them into the bathroom to clean their hands and faces, streaked with playground dirt, tears from an argument over a toy truck, and food from our picnic lunch. Ali would intercept and approve the washing of the hands but veto the face. "Leave them dirty," he'd say. Now this seemed very odd to me. Why would anyone want to make his children unattractive? My instinct was to show off my children, to dress them in the cutest clothes, comb their hair. I wanted to enhance their beauty, which deserved to be heralded I felt, not hidden. I had not yet been educated in the pervasive and menacing danger of *el'aïn*.

   At first, I thought this was just the evil eye as I understood it from the suburban Italian-American version; an old lady with a wart on her nose, dressed in black and slightly deranged, who put a curse on you for cutting through her garden or putting a baseball through her window. Growing up, a Greek neighbor used to put amputated chicken feet in the path my sister and I used when we crossed his field to get to the bus stop. I can still recall the dreadful sense of ill omen as I cut a wide arc around them.

In Tunisia, though, I soon came to understand the superstition of *el'aïn* as an important consideration in any venture -- a possible detriment to any good fortune. That tragedy can occur, not because someone wishes you ill, but because someone covets what you have, envies it, wishes desperately they could trade places with you, was a new concept to me, but it made sense. We are generally encouraged, in this culture, to make people jealous, not to underplay our successes or our good fortune, but to highlight and even exaggerate them a little. Not so in traditional Tunisian custom. Dressing up and bejeweling is only done on special occasions and even then, only after protections are in place: a pinch of black seeds, called *sinouj*, deposited in a young woman's cleavage; a tiny pillow of the same seeds, pinned into the pants lining or the dress hem of a small child. Newborn babies get shells pinned to their onesies for protection and don't get dolled up until they can walk, until their immunity against *el'aïn* is somewhat developed.

The first anniversary of our restaurant serendipitously fell on *Eid*, the end of *Ramadan*, the holy month of fasting for Muslims. Traditionally, everyone scrubs down at the *hammam* then gets all gussied up, dressed in brand new clothes purchased just for the occasion. We were in New York City, yet these little pouches of seeds appeared out of nowhere, procured from our Moroccan *maitre d'*, perhaps, or from our Senegalese sous-chef. Aziz was two years old, and I was pregnant with our second child. "Pin this into the back of Aziz's pants," Ali said, "and don't tell him." Another went into my pocket.

Protections notwithstanding, we wound up in the hospital

ER that night. Aziz had slipped and cracked his head on a wood-
en counter just as I held him, trying to prevent him from falling
off. As they examined his bulging forehead and confirmed that
he'd need stitches, the thought crossed my mind that the mysterious, non-descript pouch in the seat of his pants might rouse
some suspicions, but no one noticed. My husband was certain
that the accident was the result of *el'aïn* and reminded me of the
presence of an older woman, alone on the park bench across the
street from our apartment, who had held us in her gaze for a
long while as we walked our dog together that morning. I only
vaguely remembered the woman and had certainly not felt nervous about her presence, but Ali was not persuaded. The pouch
of seeds had been too late.

El'aïn almost always manifests in the form of freak accident
or mysterious illness. A friend of ours contracted a stomach vi-
rus last winter. He couldn't keep anything down. He had fever
and felt incredibly weak. He tried the usual teas and soups, tried
fasting, resting. After a few days he went to the doctor. The doctor prescribed some pills, more rest. After all these treatments
had failed and he was still sick, a cousin diagnosed *el'aïn* and
suggested he go see an aunt of theirs. In every Tunisian family,
there is a woman who has the ability to remove *el'aïn*. This is a
gift she is born with, and the woman of one generation will spot
it in the next and select a successor. People in the family will also
seek her out for advice. She is a household shaman of sorts, and
her wisdom is deeply respected. In our family, it turns out, that
woman was Nana.

Our friend, having run out of ideas, decided to visit his aunt.
He described the treatment to me. First, she made him lie down,
and she massaged his abdomen and joints with oil. Then she tied
a scarf around his neck and twisted it tight. Just as he was about
to lose consciousness, twitching and blue, she threw a cup of cold

water in his face and released the tourniquet. By the end of the day, all symptoms had vanished, and his energy and appetite returned. Crazy, but true, he assured me.

When we moved into our new house, we were given a bag of *sinouj* to scatter behind the cushions of the benches that line the perimeter of the living room just beyond the main entrance. This would help diffuse the feelings of envy that visitors might have upon walking into a new house. We were also given incense, with amber, frankincense, and myrrh, that we put in a special terra-cotta incense burner shaped like a fish. We put the incense on lit coals in the fish and paraded from one room to another, holding the fish above us and waving it into corners, coating each space with the beneficent smoke, sure to ward off any bad vibes.

Anything having to do with fish brings good fortune and protects against the evil eye. There are tiny jaw bones to put in your money purse, vertebrae that are pinned to a newborn's shirt or tied with pieces of string around tiny wrists. And fishtails are everywhere. There are the large tail fins of tuna, bleached by the sun and covered with dust, that are tied to grocery carts, and smaller fishtails hung from the rearview mirrors of cars to ensure safe transit. They are often affixed above the stove to protect against the misfortune of fire. Cleaning these good luck trinkets is frowned upon, lest the protective properties wear off, so they often look pretty grungy. A routine inspection of our restaurant by the NYC health department one year gave us high marks for cleanliness until the inspector spotted the old, dried salmon tail tied to the exhaust hood above the range. The inspector's hard gaze shut me down as I stumbled to explain the nature of Tunisian traditional practices, feeling myself get red in the face.

The most powerful protection, however, comes from the Koran and any of its verses. Tiny books, covered in gold leaf, are given to tuck away in the seat pockets of cars, in drawers at home, in businesses, out of sight. Longer verses are embroidered, gold or silver on black, framed, and displayed in a prominent place in the home, as high as possible. Cab drivers might have (in addition to the fishtail) a CD of prayers hanging from the rear-view mirror, or a plastic key chain with Koranic verses printed on it. These are readily available at the *souk*. Above the sink in our kitchen at home we have a hand-painted ceramic plate that says, "We begin each day with the grace of God."

And many other practices and trinkets serve the same purpose. From my mother-in-law I have learned always to put my shoes together when I take them off in the entry way, right-side up and facing in the same direction. Whenever I see one of the kids' shoes upside-down or missing its mate, I correct the situation. Shoe corralling has become part of my nightly straightening up rounds before I retire. This keeps confusion and chaos at bay, according to Nana, and who doesn't want less chaos in their lives? The forces that bring discord into the house will surely balk at such a neat row of footwear.

Other tips come from my sister-in-law: never dump dirty water out onto the earth at night, you might rouse the *j'noun*; genies, or mischievous spirits. Never clip finger nails at night for the same reason. Never argue with someone when standing in water.

Despite my education and upbringing, I find myself unable to dismiss these beliefs summarily. So, they have woven themselves surreptitiously into our day-to-day. Who knows how they came about and what effect, if any, they have on outcomes or luck, that fickle lady. No matter. The Converse All-Stars, kicked indiscriminately to the corner by my impatient kids, get lined up with our work shoes, each pair doing its part to contribute to the tranquility of our home. Because after all, who knows? Could be true...

HATA N'AÏCHU

Each and every day in my family's Tunisia begins with this question: "*Schnouah b'schnuftrou?*" What should we eat? As soon as the breakfast table is cleared, the dishes washed, and the beds made, the women of the house enjoy a last cup of coffee and discuss what to make for dinner, the main meal eaten around two o'clock. A market trip will be necessary to purchase the fresh ingredients as well as whatever staples - *zit* (oil), *melah* (salt), *ferina* (flour), *sabon* (soap) - might be in low supply.

One evening, long after supper, the *houkkah* lit and the entire family gathered on the veranda playing cards or chatting, there's a lull in the conversation. Seizing the opportunity to practice my Tunisian I blurt out: "*Schnouh b'schnuftrou hudouah?*" What will we eat tomorrow? All faces turn to me in astonishment, and sister Latifa answers, "*Wouah?! Hata n'aïchu!!*" Suddenly, everyone is laughing, belly laughing with tears streaming down their faces. It takes me a good while to get the translation from Ali: "Heh?! If we are alive tomorrow!!"

I feel equal parts embarrassed and happy to have provided

such entertainment. But at first it makes no sense to me. Why wouldn't we be as alive tomorrow as we are today? The translation of culture and mindset stumble along long after the words have been clarified, and after much confused discussion, a world of understanding suddenly opens up to me. Years of encountering panic and resistance whenever I tried to discuss plans for the future with my husband, his heightened tolerance for risk in matters of insurance, house repairs, etc., suddenly become illuminated with perfect clarity.

My husband explains to me that in the Muslim faith, God has written the story of your life, and you submit to His will in all situations. Whatever comes your way, the appropriate response is gratitude: *Hamdullah!* Before attempting any task, you invoke God's name: *Bismillah!* And you never, ever make a plan, schedule an appointment, speak of the future, without including His ultimate power: *Inch'allah!* Even something as innocuous as 'see you tomorrow' - dicey. I don't know how I feel about this as a belief, but it certainly explains a lot of the misunderstandings in our business negotiations-- and in our marriage. And I have to say, Ali is much better at being present in the moment than I am, even with my years of meditation practice.

Inch'allah incorporates the belief that life is transient, subject to sudden fluctuations of fortune. We are in God's hands. The future exists for us only if God wills it. Planning represents human hubris, potentially inviting God's wrath. We are, instead, invited to take each moment as a gift, embracing it as it comes. How different from the way I was taught to 'organize time'! I still remember the grade school writing exercise where we had to spell out 'plan ahead' across the page so that the letters came out the same size and distance from one another. For years in my relationship with Ali, I battled against what my sister dubbed 'Tunisian Time.' If the invitation said 1pm, we would argue about whether that meant we had to leave *before* 1pm (me), or *at* 1pm (Ali). Over time, we learned to compromise, but *"Hata n'aïchu"* finally solved the mystery.

Years later, in nursing school, I am reminded of this evening during a lecture on culturally appropriate patient care. Muslims, we learn, may find it challenging to sign a consent form before a procedure. A medical consent outlines the possible risks of the procedure and asks the patient to confirm that he understands and accepts these risks, including the possibility of death. Of course, Muslims are an incredibly diverse population and often highly educated. Nonetheless, *hata n'aïchu* may be sitting on their shoulder as the patient signs their name.

THE STAFF OF LIFE

Hobbous. A meal without bread would be unthinkable in Tunisia. Before the table is set, as the food is nearing the end of its preparation, one or two of the children are sent out to buy anywhere from three to eight *baguettes*, the standard loaf since the French colonists brought it here in the nineteenth century. One can buy either *baguettes* or *hobbous*, a slightly wider version of the *baguette*, of the same length and made with the same dough. The other option is the traditional, Tunisian *tabouna*, a round, flat bread, dimpled and heavy, made in a clay oven that looks like a small open-mouthed volcano. It is a denser, chewier loaf, made from semolina and far superior to the others as far as I'm concerned. But it is often only available in the artisan bakeries, and every corner store sells the French bread. Tunisian *baguettes* are often a clumsy imitation of the French, but have nearly replaced the native *tabouna*. This fairly common aspect of post-colonial life, I imagine, is not limited to just the bread.

Colonists introduced many foods and practices that remained after they had left. Native Tunisians resisted some and

embraced others, though not always successfully. There is a re-
naissance of pre-colonial artisan and culinary tradition in Tunisia today, but it seems, like so many treasures from that country,
intended more for the pleasure of the knowledgeable tourist who
can afford it than for the average Tunisian.

At the same time, most educated Tunisians are scrambling
to distance themselves from their traditions. So many have immigrated to Europe or Canada, about five million, compared
to about the eleven million living in Tunisia itself. For many of
them, the question of identity is complex, particularly in light
of recent political and historical events and the changing world
view of Arabs and Muslims. Tunisian immigrants of my generation struggled to assimilate into the cultures that adopted them,
often to the detriment of their own traditions and language.

In Tunisia, as well, educated and affluent seems to mean European. Gigantic French supermarkets, selling everything from
packaged foods to clothing and furniture, attract the two-income
young families who refuse traditional wedding ceremonies and
consult French decorating magazines even as the German tourists purchase hand-painted tiles with ancient motifs to cover their
entryways at home. Herbal remedies used successfully for centuries and passed down from mother to daughter are eschewed
for antibiotics and cortisone creams for the slightest ailment, the
labels all printed in French. It breaks my heart to witness my
teenaged nieces refuse *henna* before their cousin's engagement
party, looking on as our Canadian-American-German-Tunisian
daughters and I get ours done.

Most often it is the teenaged nieces who go out on the bread
errand. Clean shirts are found, hair quickly smoothed back with
water to freshen the ponytail, an approving glance in the mirror,
and they're off. In the small town where we live, the closest store
is a ten-minute walk. Time enough to gossip in private, to spread

wings and contemplate the possibility of an encounter on the way or in the store, which is run by two very handsome young men. I have witnessed the pronounced difference in the way the merchants speak to me, polite but reserved, and the way they speak to my nieces and our older daughters. Though the words might be the same, the exchange of goods for money identical, the meaning, the subtext, is a world apart. Their eyes seem to acquire a different shape and depth of color. Our young women are at the threshold of another realm, but they visit it in complete safety. They are only buying bread, after all. They will return, thirty minutes later, with an extra swing in their gait, a light in their eyes, which they consciously modify as they enter the door. Their mothers are acutely sensitive to any changes in their children's behavior. Trouble is detected almost by scent long before it has a chance to blossom. Not so long ago they themselves were sent out to get the bread, after all.

The bread is laid out on the table, but not all of it. As with the copious quantities of food we have prepared, the matriarch will dole out limited amounts at a time, never fully revealing how much is left. When we cook, we cook for twice the number of people, generally between ten and fifteen on any given day. There needs to be enough for visitors, after all, if they appear, and for leftovers which will add variety to the next meal. And then, Tunisians want to eat well at mealtimes, because snacking is unheard of, unless you are a mother, "tasting" as she cooks, or a very young child. So, serving dishes are filled in the kitchen, and modest portions doled out by the matriarch. The bread will fill out the meal, serving as accompaniment, utensil, and sponge. As needed, more bread will be retrieved from the canvas bread bag that hangs from a doorknob, the serving dishes refilled from the mother lode in the kitchen. In this way generosity, fairness, and economy are maintained in balance at the table, in the family, and in the kitchen.

Tunisian food consists largely of stews or dishes made with tiny pasta or *couscous* or rice, along with finely chopped salads, so spoons are generally the only utensils required at the table. And bread. Most Tunisians use a spoon for soup or *couscous* only and use bread for the rest. This is not a practice to be attempted casually. Some instruction and a great deal of patient practice and encouragement are required. You must use only the right hand, and only the thumb and first two fingers of that hand. The reasons for this are twofold: left-handedness is still discouraged in most families as indicative of wayward behavior with the potential to invite or attract discord and chaos; also, the left hand is traditionally reserved for aspects of personal hygiene to be kept strictly separate from eating. Any other way of holding the bread is as frowned upon as we in the US would do if someone slurped his soup or held his fork in his fist.

A small piece of bread is torn from the larger piece that sits next to your plate. It's best to have a piece that has just a little of the *mie* attached to the crust, or to take just the *mie*, if that's what you prefer, and flatten it. This will make for better scooping. Then you place the bread carefully onto a bite-sized quantity of food at the edge of the portion and gently but firmly draw it to the edge of the plate. All Tunisian food is served in shallow bowls to facilitate this technique. Now you quickly move your thumb from the bread to trap the food at the edge of the plate and tamp it against the bread. Then you deftly flip it upright and put it in your mouth. Those who are most experienced at this technique will not even want a napkin but will discretely suck any remaining sauce from their thumb from time to time at the end of a bite. My attempts have met with varying degrees of success, but I am still dependent on my spoon, and my hands, both of them, are a mess at the end of the meal. Still, my wonderful family is patient and lovingly shows me again and again when I ask for help - and graciously ignores my failures.

After the meal, crumbs and odd ends of bread, too small to save for the next meal, litter the table. Nothing is ever discarded. A fundamental principal of Islam, as my sisters explain, is the importance of not being wasteful. God is bountifully generous, and to waste is to disrespect that generosity in the most blatant way. Bread has become the ultimate symbol of this relationship, and so we sweep the crumbs out to feed the birds and gather the smaller ends in plastic bags. From time to time, people in need come through the neighborhood, collecting these bags from one house to the next. They in turn sell the bread to shepherds or donkey-cart drivers, who feed it to their animals. No waste. We all partake in the bounty and share it with others down the line. I have also seen this kind of sharing done with clothes and with furniture.

I have seen clothes worn until they are unwearable. The two or three changes of outfit for each of the two seasons are washed and ironed, washed again, and mended until they are thread-bare. But sometimes there are children's clothes that have been outgrown with no one to inherit them or adult clothes that no longer fit and can't be adjusted at the tailor's. Or else, someone has passed away and no one really wants to wear those clothes. These, too, get wrapped up in bundles and given to the poor who solicit for them through the neighborhood. They will clean them once more and sell them, neatly folded, on sheets spread out at the *souk*.

In the same way, it would be unthinkable to throw away fur-niture. There is certainly a cousin who can use it, or an old aunt. The flea market on the edge of the city is full of these used items, for sale at a nominal price. You never see usable furniture outside to be collected by the garbage. This would be considered *haram*, sinful, as if the bounty that made it possible for you to discard the table, the jacket, the bread, were not a gift from heaven, but something within your control, something you could take for granted.

When we break the end of the fresh bread and relish it, anticipating the family meal, or when we toast up yesterday's bread over the open flame of the stove in the morning and slather on some quince jam, we bring an awareness of where that bread comes from and all that it represents –the market where we bought it, the country's history, the coming of age of our daughters, and the affirmation that life is generous, and precious, and meant to be shared.

WATER I

From the women, who have been educated by their mothers and grandmothers, I learn the special meaning and powers of water. It can both transmit disease and heal the body. It has sensitivity and intelligence. It can communicate feelings and thought, expressions of energy that become amplified and travel more quickly in the liquid element.

As a prelude to each of the five daily prayers, Muslims wash hands, face, and feet, divesting themselves of the accumulated dust of body and mind before they address God. How beautiful, I think. Here are the parts that do and make, that see and hear and smell, that speak and engage with the world, the parts that walk on the earth. Washing these portals to the world is a way of opening the door, of crossing a threshold from the mundane into the sacred. If there is no water, a Muslim may use sand as a stand-in. If there's no sand, they may strike the earth and go through the motions. The hands curl rhythmically around each other, splashing imaginary water onto the face, eyes squeezed shut, scooping it around the ears, in a trance-like dance. Intend the water, and you will be cleansed.

There are many superstitions and traditions surrounding water. On the seventh day of a child's life, for example, he or she is given a special bath. The mother selects from her family and acquaintances a young person of vibrant energy, someone who embodies the qualities which the mother wishes for her child. This person then takes the used water from the baby's bath and, singing and dancing, spills it out into the street in front of the house, discarding whatever bad spirits might have been hanging around the child's soul, inviting fresh and joyous ones instead.

In general, one should be mindful of negativity around water. It is considered particularly bad luck to argue with someone while immersed in water, for example, or to reprimand a child while bathing in the sea. I'm advised never to dump dirty dishwater at night, when the *jnoun* are resting in the earth and might be roused to anger or mischief. When cleaning fish or meat, we spill the blood-streaked water slowly, carefully, and with conscious reverence for the life that has been spent. My sister, the one who goes into a trance when the drums play at family celebrations, says *bismillah* as the scarlet blood slips down the drain.

Tunisia, like many Arab-speaking countries, is dry and hot, and water is the reviver, the savior, the purifier. There is nothing absent-minded about how people use water here. It provides an invitation to grace, an opening of sorts. Whenever water is enjoyed, there is an aspect of sweet reverence and joyful abundance. And yet, it is never wasted. When my sister washes her hands, I am mesmerized by her gestures. The water seems to take on a mercurial quality, acquiring different physical properties as it touches her hands. It moves over them with a kind of oily heaviness; it refracts light with a particular brilliance. She pivots her wrists, cups her hands, folds them over each other in one graceful, fluid gesture, her long, smooth fingers perfectly parallel. I

DOROTHEA BIBA NAOUAI · 99

am struck by the beauty of her hands in this element, and how her skin seems not to have been in the least ravaged by it, despite her age. You would never guess that she plunges her bare hands into water countless times each day, washing everything by hand, including sheets and towels. She washes with bleach, with caustic soaps, with lemons squeezed into the dishwater to combat the smell of eggs or fish. I have to protect my hands from water and its damaging effects with rubber gloves, special emollients. And still, the element has not been kind to me, my hands look parched next to hers. She has washed her hands this way since earliest childhood, with the same reverence, the same grace. This simple gesture is rife with meaning for her. The cleansing of the hands, the body, a bowl of fruit, has its echo in the spirit. It calls up gratitude and offers quiet reprieve from the activities of the day. Perhaps I can learn this. I start by putting away the gloves.

WATER II

At the beach, there are several kinds of bathers of the feminine variety to behold. Most immediately visible are the modern, younger women, often the children of Tunisians who have immigrated to Europe and return for the summer. Their bikinis are as itsy bitsy as they might be in Nice or St. Tropez, and the girls are hardly self-conscious about wearing something their mother's generation would have considered illicit. As a concession to these mothers, however, they might wear a *cache-maillot*, a silk scarf wrapped around the hips, or a clingy spaghetti-strapped dress, a loose gesture of modesty or deference. The hips and thighs seem to be considered the danger zones here, inviting more lustful glances than cleavage, which is often prominently displayed. The girls' heads are bare, and thick black curls cascade down bronze backs and shoulders. They seem to be fully aware of their stunning beauty as they skip and splash noisily in the surf, to the utter delight and delirium of the young men who chase after them.

Of another category and equally mesmerizing are the women

who choose to remain in traditional bathing dress. In this category there are two kinds; the first, generally women just past child-bearing age, wear short-sleeved *jelabas*, straight-cut simple robes, printed with brightly colored floral or tie-dye patterns. Their hair is gathered in equally vibrant and mismatched headscarves, which they wear turban-style, tied around the head. They look like festive gypsies and seem totally at home in their bathing gear. To my eyes, they embody a kind of freedom from self-consciousness that I have never known, an inner strength bred from life and living.

The second group of traditionally dressed women wear long, crêpe *jelabas* which extend just past the wrists and ankles. They are usually somber or neutral in color and gracefully embroidered around the cuffs, hem, and neckline of the dress in thread the same color as the cloth. These are worn by the more religious women who strictly follow the Muslim traditions regarding modesty. Their hair and bosoms, ankles and wrists must be covered at all times, and the fabric of their garment should be neither form-fitting nor transparent. Their robes move easily in the breeze, and the fabric dances and billows about their feminine silhouettes. These women cover their heads with the more conservative *hijab*, a dark head scarf of one color, unadorned, which gets pinned under the chin, revealing only the oval of the face itself. They look beautiful and majestic, like mysterious, untouchable nobility. They carry themselves in a way that troubles any notions about the restrictiveness of women's dress in the Arab world, and about oppression and freedom.

Unlike the modern women, whose movements are jubilant as they frolic and splash in the water, the traditionally dressed women wade in slowly, one foot placed gently in front of the other, like goddesses returning to the sea. Their bearing is completely different from their younger counterparts, and perhaps their experience of the water as well, judging by their expressions. They seem to be merging with the water, welcoming its embrace. As their dresses balloon out, then sink down, then float about them, their hands fan out, making wide arcs on the surface of the water. They will go in to their shoulders and may stay submerged this way for a long time while they laugh and chat with other women. When they come back to shore, with the same steady walk, I am amazed that they don't seem in the least irritated by the yards of wet fabric that now cling to their bodies. After a time, I understand that while I, in my lycra bathing suit, am dried off and scorched again within minutes, their garments keep them cool for a long while as they sit on the shore and gaze out at the rippling sea.

WATER III

Here are three things you cannot do easily without a bowl of water handy:

1) peel *hindi* (the prickly cactus fruit), with its invisible spines;
2) peel garlic, especially Tunisian garlic, which has impossibly tiny cloves that are covered with a bluish-purple, tenacious skin;
3) roll miniature lamb meat balls, seasoned with mint or garlic and cumin, to add to a soup or *tagine*.

These already labor-intensive tasks become impossible with sticky fingers. Everything is made easier with a bowl of cool water nearby. If the hands or the garlic are kept wet, for example, the skins slide off into the water and the cleaned garlic forms a small heap in no time, fingers free and clean to peel the next one. These are things you can only learn in a Tunisian kitchen on a hot summer morning, surrounded by patient and loving aunts.

WATER IV

This is how we say goodbye. When the summer is over it is time for us to return to the US. The day beforehand, we make frantic, last-minute runs to the *souk* for bags of *henna* or hand-painted ceramic bowls or tiny souvenirs to bring back to friends and family: straw hand-held fans one year, tiny red and yellow cans of *harissa* the next, or big cooking spoons, carved from a single piece of wood. A gigantic sendoff meal is prepared at home, and from late afternoon the visitors trickle in. Some stay just for tea and a quick goodbye, some bring bags or boxes of pastries for loved ones in the US, but many will stay the night and keep the party going until we leave for our flight in the early morning.

At five AM, we tiptoe over the sleeping guests, laid out like sardines on floor mats and couches. We haul our suitcases out to the two friends with cars who have come to take us to the airport. The children are sleepy from having stayed up so late, and we are saturated with the nostalgia of summer's end and teary goodbyes. The sisters, always awake to preside over the departure and make the morning coffee, stand together in the small doorway of the house, a pail of water in their hands.

As we pull away, they throw the water out after the departing cars and their passengers, travelers, loved ones who left and came back and are leaving again. I turn to watch them and just catch the sweep of the bucket, the bright slap of water on the dusty car and pavement, a gesture offered as a kind of good luck charm for our imminent return. I only really understand it after a number of years, the first time I hold the bucket for guests of ours who are leaving, the first summer we stay in our own house: The cyclical nature of water, always leaving always returning, tides advancing and retreating, evaporation and rainfall, water tables and oceans, traveling between continents, connecting their separate and distant land masses. Water always returns, one day, to the source from whence it came.

WATER V

Where is she from? Somewhere in the country, perhaps Tata-ouine (think Star Wars underground desert caves) or Matmata? Definitely not Tunis, with her colorful layers of patterned scarves and blouses and skirts. Plastic *shlekas* on her feet. Hair wrapped in a flowered turban, a few locks peeking out, bright orange from *henna*. Gold bangles on her wrist. She carries nothing save per-haps some money tucked into her brassiere or a hidden pocket in her skirt. She's incongruous on this crowded tram in the heart of Tunis on this melting-hot summer day. She is alone, but not afraid. Her eyes sparkle, shine like gems from a dark honeyed face that is so deeply wrinkled it takes me a minute to distinguish nose, lips, eyelids. Just below her cheekbones, barely visible, I no-tice two faded green-grey tattoos of geometric designs. Yes, she must be from the country. Who knows what her mission is here in the city today. How did she get here, alone? She may not even know how to read Arabic, let alone French. If she is the daughter of a shepherd, for example, she may have been birthed under the stars and never even seen the inside of a hospital or bank or school. She may not have a birth certificate or carry identification of any kind. She may not know her exact age. This would not be unusual for someone of her generation who hails from the deep country.

And yet, here she is, just as are we - Ali, myself, the children - sweating, waiting out the time in transportation, going from and to. She catches my eye and smiles. A radiant smile. No teeth, but the warmth of the sun, the earth, fills her face, her gaze. She says something in a raspy voice. I don't understand, I look at Ali. He smiles and explains that she is asking for water. I look at the two-liter bottle of Evian in my hands, precious commodity. I hesitate for the briefest second, considering my western habit of sanitary concerns, knowing about germs, microscopes, contagion, etc. I look back at her and she is still beaming. She knows we will share and is glad to gift us the opportunity to be generous, that prized Tunisian quality. I hand her the bottle and her dry, calloused hands brush mine, no hesitation, no awkwardness. A jolt of energy in the contact and then warmth. She takes the bottle, nearly half her size, and unscrews the cap. With utmost celebratory reverence, she wipes the mouth of the bottle, whispers *bismillah,* and brings it to her lips. A long draught, skinny neck and mandible working to take in the refreshing water. After she's done, another wipe and she replaces the cap. Her face shines back at ours as she returns the plastic bottle. *Bishfeh! Ishfik!*

WASHING I

Many Tunisians opt out of heated water at home to save on the cost of fuel. So, they make do with frigid sponge baths and treat themselves to the *hammam* once a week or so. *Hammam* are Roman or Turkish baths: communal, steam-heated bathing rooms with different temperatures, hot, cold, and medium, and with running hot and cold water to wash with. In the suburb of Bardo, where my sister, Latifa, lives, the *hammam* is quite modern. It has the feel of a community swimming pool, but is more inviting, with decorative tiles from floor to ceiling. Today, a hot August day, we have come together, Latifa, my daughter Aicha, and I, to wash away the grime and dirt of six weeks spent at the beach with never enough hot water for our extended family. I have been to the *hammam* several times, but this is a first for Aicha, who is six, and who loves water and bathing in any form.

We walk from Latifa's house armed with bags of soaps and exfoliating gloves, combs and brushes, clean towels, and a fresh change of clothes. We secure a spot for ourselves in the resting room, a large pillared space with an elevated area around the perimeter which is covered with straw mats and punctuated by colorful pillows. This is where we will get changed and where we will relax after we finish washing and steaming. As modern as it is, it distinctly recalls the atmosphere of the *harem* paintings by 19th century French artists. As we strip down to our underpants, we hear ululating and see a small group of women exit from the baths. A bride is being prepared for her wedding night. The party moves off to a separate, private room, where they will have cakes and tea and tell stories of wedding nights past while they *henna* her hair, hands, and feet, and wax her hairless from cheek to toe.

We take our washing paraphernalia and enter through a fogged glass door into the baths themselves. An aide hands us a stack of colorful plastic buckets. She is in her late fifties at least, of generous and solid proportions, and wears a lacy black slip over an amply brassiered bosom, her hair gathered under a printed cotton scarf that encloses her head like a turban. Her plastic slippers, her *shlekas*, make a clacking sound as she shuffles from one part of the baths to the other. She works here all day and seems impervious to the heat. She supplies the bathers with buckets, squeegees excess water from the tiled floors and, for a fee, will scrub you down if you are unfortunate enough to have come alone.

In the past, the matron of the *hammam* was a very powerful figure in Tunisian society, a kind of marriage broker. She knew all the families in the neighborhood. She also knew the personal and social habits, not to mention the physical attributes and hygiene practices, of each and every woman therein. When it was time for a mother to find an appropriate mate for her son, there was no better person to consult than the *hammam* lady – observant, all-knowing, connected. Today, these women still carry an air of quiet power about them. I can feel the scrutiny in her gaze, imagine the conversations that happen once the doors have closed.

After securing a spot, we set to work filling our buckets from rows of spigots in the hottest room. We fill some buckets with hot water and some with cold to mix and wash with. We test the water continuously with our hands, scooping and decanting from one bucket to the next until the temperatures are deemed just right. We bring the filled buckets into the medium room and set ourselves up, spreading our paraphernalia out on the bench.

What a sight! This is a veritable Fellini buffet. Women of all ages, shapes, and sizes decorate the foggy room. Most of the bodies are of ample proportions and there is no attempt to hide or minimize. Like the lines of a palm, the bodies reveal the lives that have been lived in them: the flawlessly smooth and graceful bodies of the youngest women, luxuriating in the knowledge of their own beauty and completely unaware that it will transform; the filled out and generous bodies of the mothers, breasts and abdomens full of life's purpose fulfilled, some grossly scarred from caesareans or appendices removed; the older women, skin beginning to separate from flesh, breasts heavy and pendulous, joints swollen with arthritis and overuse. None of these women has heard of sculpting abs or yoga butt or entertained the notion of plastic surgery. Their daily chores are full of exercise of every kind and rest is welcome, pampering deserved.

With very few exceptions, no one is alone. Small groups of three or four women help each other wash, scrubbing with rough exfoliating gloves once the steam has taken effect and the skin is soft. One braces herself, palms pushed against the wall, arms straight, and the other scrubs. Then they switch. Great delight is expressed in how much dead skin gets sloughed off in the process and rinsed away. We do the same and rinse off with warm water, mixed in one of the buckets, scooped out with a pale-blue plastic heart-shaped ladle. Our skin is squeaky clean (we have tested it) and varying shades of pink and brown.

The first time I went to a *hammam*, on our very first trip to Tunisia, my husband's sisters took me, all five of them together. I was being checked out, for sure, put to the test. They were all very helpful and insisted on taking turns scrubbing me with the glove. My only faux pas, immediately checked and corrected, was to take off my underwear and apply body lotion in full view of the other ladies in the dressing room. That evening when we got home, one of my future sisters exclaimed triumphantly that I had been filthy! She had never imagined that such a pale-skinned woman could produce such quantities of black skin.

Tunisian women are encouraged to remove all body hair "from here to here" - *hakka ou hakka* - as one cousin says, gesturing with a final chop between her feet and her forehead. They do this with a wax made at home from melted sugar and fresh lemon juice, beginning in puberty. The aesthetic of a perfectly hairless body must be completely realized by a woman's wedding night. In the *hammam*, this gives the women an extra slickness and, for a moment, their curvaceous shapes and the sheen of their skin make them look for all the world like sea lions basking in the sun.

Indeed, this quality of well-being permeates the *hammam*. Women's time is in the late afternoon, when chores have been finished, husbands and children fed and placated. For the next two hours they will be their own and each other's sole concern, giving and receiving a myriad of small but tender attentions. Friends and neighbors are encountered, news exchanged, and, after the effects of the pampering have begun to soften the defenses, concerns and hopes shared. The physical self-consciousness that I have witnessed and experienced in saunas in America and Europe is hard to find here. Instead, the body, whatever its size, shape, or evident history, is cleansed, massaged, anointed, with the greatest love and care, in an atmosphere of recreation and quiet indulgence.

Lastly, we wash and condition our hair in the cool room. Aicha, as if bewitched, can't stop filling buckets and has become the *hammam* matron's assistant, distributing them to all the customers. The containers are half her size and heavy, but she hauls them with great energy, her red cheeks puffing, her brow furrowed in determination. A little boy comes by for the third or fourth time and stares at me. I am the wrong color, the wrong shape. He looks a little dazed and seems very familiar with everything. I wonder if he is related to one of the employees here and how much time he has spent in the steam.

We exit, and the summer air of the tiled resting room seems refreshingly cool. We sit wrapped in towels for a while, taking in the after-effects of the steam and enjoying the sensation of utter peace and profound *detente*. We are satiated with pampering. We purchase lukewarm bottled sodas with unfamiliar flavors – apple, tamarind, mint – and sip them slowly. As we dress, a family of five women next to us discusses the fiancée of a cousin, and their opinions are easy to read on the animated faces, even though I understand only every third or fourth word: disapproval, predictions of certain heartache and regret. Lotions are sniffed and hairbrushes passed around, help exchanged with zippers and necklace fastenings. With some reluctance, we take leave of the *hammam* and the outside world reclaims us.

At home, we compare notes with Ali and his father, who took our two boys. Aziz and Khalil, aged ten and eight, were fascinated and enchanted and have many stories to tell. Their grandfather, who is blind, had insisted on scrubbing them himself and they animatedly mimic how he did it: holding them by the wrist, leaning in to scrub their arms with the glove, testing for effectiveness by running his shaky pale fingers along their skinny brown arms. They tell me about the special towels they were given to wrap around their waists and show me how they were folded over so as not to slip. They describe the big, burly man who was assigned to massage their father by walking on his back. They had gone to the old neighborhood *hammam* in Tunis, constructed ages ago from big slabs of stone. The older baths are dark and gloomy, dense with hovering steam and a slightly dank smell. The atmosphere there encourages the active imagination and, indeed, *hammam* tales abound, generally involving *jnoun* - genies, mischievous spirits - and my father-in-law proceeds to tell us this one:

The men's *hammam* opens at 6am but it is never advisable to be the first one in alone. *Jnoun* take up residence at night and are happy to confuse and torture a lone soul in the early hours of the morning. Nonetheless, on the day on which this story takes place, a middle-aged man goes to the *hammam* first thing in the morning and upon arriving, is warned by the *hammam* keeper that there is no one in the baths and that he might consider waiting or returning with a friend. The customer laughs it off and insists that he doesn't believe in *jnoun*, and that, in any case, this is the only time he has available to enjoy the baths. The keeper lets him in reluctantly and equips him with the necessary towels and buckets. Upon entering, the customer sees two older gentlemen sitting together. He goes to them, happy for the company and says, "Funny, the guy said there was no one here. Mind if I join you?"

"Sure. We've been here for a while," they say. After a time, the customer looks over and sees the nose of one of the men melting slowly to the ground. He rubs his eyes, sure his sleepy state and the steam have conspired to play tricks on him. Again, he looks over and sees the man's nose stretched halfway to the ground.

His companion seems to notice nothing unusual. Frantically, he says to him, "Please, look at that man's nose! Do you see what it's doing? Something is terribly wrong! His nose is melting to the floor!"

At this, my father-in-law pauses, listens to make sure everyone is paying attention. His eyebrows are raised, his milky eyes wide open. We are hanging in suspense. Then he becomes the other man, who responds, "What do you mean? Like this?" and with a devilish grin, he grabs his nose and pantomimes stretching it out a few feet from his face, a maniacal Pinocchio. At this, the story concludes, the customer runs screaming in fright as fast as his legs can take him, out of the *hammam* and away from the *jnoun*. My father-in-law relishes our exclamations of surprise and horror. He is adept at sensing what he cannot see, and he can tell that he has hit his mark. Tunisians are born storytellers and the singular atmosphere of the *hammam* is fresh in our minds.

WASHING II

This is how we wash our clothes: First, the clothes are gathered and separated into light and dark piles. Three colorful, plastic buckets big enough for my toddler to play in are then brought outside to the courtyard, where all the washing is done in the summer. The hose is turned on, and the powdered soap is added and agitated with a practiced hand, fingers spread wide. This is the same soap we use for dishwashing and for all manner of house-cleaning, a generic, powdered soap with blue flecks. The clothes are added, and rhythmically drawn in and out of the suds. The courtyard is filled with summer light, jasmine vines climb the walls and birds flit back and forth, across the wide, open sky. This is not even remotely related to the basement laundry room back home. Stubborn stains are treated with a bar of olive oil soap, rubbed into the stain and left in the sun to take. A turmeric stain of a deep golden yellow, will turn a bright magenta first, then fade entirely. The clothes are let to soak for a while, while other chores are tended to. Twenty minutes later, the hose is turned on again and left in another bucket for rinsing. During this time, the clothes are agitated again, and I struggle to mirror the fluidity of the gestures that my husband's sisters have acquired over time.

Once all the suds have disappeared from the water and the courtyard is refreshingly drenched with the overflow, the hose is turned off and the wringing out and hanging up begins. This is possibly my favorite part, requiring some strength but a great deal more ingenuity. Watching me wring out a pair of pants, Latifa, observing with a keen eye, shakes her head and advises me to use less effort, lest I tire out my hands; the sun will evaporate whatever water I don't squeeze from the clothes.

Everything must be turned inside out, to protect the garments from fading by the bleaching effect of the sun. While she works, Latifa drapes a damp shirt over her head for air conditioning. I do the same. The relief is instantaneous. The smaller items are no problem, and are quickly pinned to the wash line, underwear draped over the curls of the blue iron window guards, so as not to waste precious clothespins. The bath towels and the bed sheets are a different matter. These, if you have no one to help you, are quite tricky, as they are heavy with water and bulky in size. Seeing me struggle one morning, Latifa shows me the trick: You hold one end of the sheet or towel with the other end still in the water, and swirl it in one direction (clockwise or counterclockwise). The top of the sheet (or towel) has twisted itself and you can now wring it out very easily from the top down. Fantastic! The sight of so many clothes and linen, billowing in the warm morning breeze, the cool sensation of wet legs, arms and skirt hems quickly drying, fills my heart with pride and delight.

WASHING III

Here is how we wash the floor: Shoes and toys are lifted onto the couches and beds, chairs put upside down on tables, rugs rolled out of the way and banged onto their ends in the courtyard outside. The floor is swept, debris pushed onto an impromptu dustpan made from a piece of cardboard. Then buckets of water with a little bleach added are brought in,. The women, barefoot, tuck their skirts into their underpants, leaving their legs exposed and giving them the appearance of pirates wearing pantaloons and head scarves, gold earrings dangling.

The buckets of water are splashed out onto the floor with a smooth, sweeping gesture. The wet floor is then scrubbed with a broom, vigorously. Any remaining dust, food debris, candy wrappers, sunflower seed shells, and dead insects all swim about in the increasingly dirty puddles. Then the squeegee, essentially a window-washer's tool, comes out, and the water is pulled out towards the nearest exit. In every house, the floors are tiled, and they slope gently either towards a drain in the middle of the floor or towards the doors to the outside. I have never seen this chore done differently, and it is always a party. This activity inevitably brings my children running, fighting over who gets to wield the squeegee.

WASHING IV

This is how we wash Nana. As Nana grew old, the attentions of her daughters sometimes irritated her. She who had cared so well for so many now needed to be cared for, and this upset her. She often pushed food away, complaining that the sauce was too *haar* (spicy), the fruit too *chares* (sour). It was difficult for her to walk and getting her to agree to bathe became a real struggle, even in the summer. Sometimes, the daughters could cajole her into going to the beach in the afternoon and wade with her, two on either side, into the shallow, turquoise Mediterranean. Otherwise, they would plead with Ali to reason with her when it was time for a bath or a trip to the *hammam*. This he did willingly, and he was often successful in convincing her-- or else she consented just to make him happy.

On one occasion, however, she wouldn't budge. We had rented a house in the seaside town where eventually we would build our own. She was sitting on one of the terraces, enjoying the morning and the perfume of mint and sage from the garden. After several tries, her children seemed to have given up on her, and she was pleased with herself. Unknown to her, Ali had gone around to the back of the house to retrieve the long garden hose, which was connected to a well of fresh, cool water. Quietly, stealthily, he wound around until he was just around the corner from where she sat. Three sisters lay in wait behind the terrace door, soap and washcloths, towels and fresh clothes at the ready. Another sister turned the hose on, and suddenly the entire household was alerted to Nana's surprise shower by her cries for mercy.

The children and I ran out to find mother and grown children laughing and squealing and crying and washing. Later, clean and dry and reclining inside on the sofa for her siesta, she complained with just a touch of satisfaction that the bath had given her an awful chill, that she had been tortured by her ungrateful children. Exempt from her recriminations, I covered her with a heavy woolen blanket and kissed her forehead, and she soon fell fast asleep.

THE CEMETERY

It's nearing the end of summer. The days are heavy with heat and unprecedented humidity. We go to market as early as we can. The children droop like wilted leaves and argue for the first time in weeks. Nonetheless, we have decided to visit Nana's grave together. The night before, we prepare a bag: empty two-liter plastic water bottles, head scarves, a bag of bird seed. We eat a modest dinner of leftovers. Afterwards, while we are washing the dishes, Latifa hesitates, then tells me to stay quiet tonight. She looks directly into my eyes, blushes a little. I understand her meaning without elaboration. We are to keep all our carnal appetites in check in preparation for our pilgrimage tomorrow, out of respect for the dead.

In the morning we wash, get dressed, and eat our breakfast. I have to stifle the kids' complaints – "Do we *have* to go to Nana's grave?" – and explain to them that visiting her together is one way of remembering her. The year that Nana died, I also lost my own grandmother Helena. She had lived in Berkeley, California, and we went together as a family to her memorial. The honoring of the dead is enigmatic to most children, who are so busy living. They haven't yet understood that these rituals of remembrance are less for the dead than for those who remain as they struggle to weave over the void left by a loved one.

From my husband and his sisters, I learn that, in their tradition, there is a specific schedule to visit the grave after a burial-first after three days, then after one week, then after one month, etc., until one year has passed. During that first week, a candle is kept lit in the window, to orient the soul to its earthly home as it wanders before it transitions. The family brings meals to the neighborhood mosque at regular intervals in the name of the deceased. During that first year, the family is expected to stay home and decline all invitations to celebrate weddings or circumcisions or to go to the beach They will also postpone those events in their own extended family.

We take two taxis with my husband, Latifa, myself, my niece, and our five children. Already the day is a scorcher. A kind of stagnant mist hangs in the air, blurring the edges of things. We are on the outskirts of the city, and smog from the many automobiles mixes with the dust, making it difficult to breathe.

We arrive at the cemetery. We pass through the gate of the plain whitewashed concrete wall, about four feet high, that marks the perimeter. The cemetery is on a hillside, and as we look up from the entrance, we are greeted by the sight of hundreds of white gravestones, a few trees, and winding paths. We fill our water bottles from spigots at an all-purpose building that houses the maintenance and administrative offices. Cemeteries are not private enterprises here. While it is possible to purchase larger family plots or embellishments to the grave, this is generally considered prideful, and therefore *haram*. Death is the ultimate equalizer, and humility before your maker is seen as a virtue.

Some visitors pray in the space in front of the building.

Beggars crouch, hands outstretched. Some have pre-filled water bottles to offer. There is no set price. Your sense of generosity is appealed to, and for each person, this is different. Latifa gives me a head scarf, and one for her daughter and for our teenaged daughters as well. She helps us drape them over our heads, then loosely around our shoulders.

All morning an atmosphere of solemnity has prevailed. Throughout breakfast, in the taxicab on the way to the cemetery, hardly a word was spoken. Now, as we walk up the hilly, winding slope, other emotions take hold. We feel sadness and anticipation, an unspoken communication between us. Another sister and her daughter have joined us, and we are a family going to pay our respects to the woman who was the strong, steady trunk of the tree. Two years after her death, her children struggle still to maintain the unity that was a given during her life. No one remaining has Nana's energy and sheer force of will, but we are making this trip in her name and everyone is glad to be participating.

We arrive at her grave. Muslims are buried directly into the earth, "dust to dust," wrapped only in a simple cloth, the *soutr,* or shroud. Each of Nana's children carries a small square of this cloth, the last to have touched her body, as a talisman, a reminder. The grave is marked by a simple slab of whitewashed concrete with a small blue ceramic cup embedded in the center, just where her heart would be. The marble tombstone is sparsely engraved with the details of her birth and death and a simple verse from the Koran. As embellishments, Nana's children chose only two small benches, placed flanking the grave. We sit on these now, though they could almost have been made for children, and we are pressed together. Some remain standing.

Nana's grave is situated towards the top of the cemetery, with an expansive view over all the rest and beyond, into the city. The hundreds of white graves are tightly scattered and look almost like a handful of pebbles strewn by a child. There is none of the geometrical rigor of cemeteries in the States, and these graves are so much closer together. A drier, coarser version of a European weeping willow tree graces the site, just beyond her tombstone. The long, fingerlike branches fan out to welcome us. I can't help thinking that she wound up with a particularly nice spot, and we imagine that she likes it here.

We begin by washing the grave and tombstone with the water we have carried with us. As we pour we caress the stone, the concrete, with our hands until the grave is cleansed of dust. But we are washing her also, refreshing her soul, nourishing and reviving her in our hearts. Her children talk to her as they move the water over the stone, and a few have already begun to weep openly. The last of the water is poured into the cup in the center of the slab. This is for the birds, as is the seed, which we scatter liberally on her grave and the graves that surround hers. The feeding and fluttering of birds will keep her company once we have left. We sit in stillness now and bow our heads. Our palms are cupped above her grave in a gesture of acceptance as Latifa recites a prayer. We are all crying now, save the children, who look on in wonder. The loss is tangible as we visit her again, the desire to live up to her legacy renewed.

This is the second time I have visited her grave. At my husband's request, we did not go with him to the funeral. Muslim tradition dictates burial within twenty-four hours, so we had to organize our lives quickly. He was also worried that the intense display of grief would shock and frighten our children. Indeed, his accounts of the funeral and burial were unlike the Episcopalian and agnostic funerals I had attended. Loud and passionate demonstrations of grief, loss of consciousness, thronging masses of friends and relations, and none of the restraint to which we in the West are accustomed. But I regret not going, and not bringing our children as well, and the regret wells up in me again now. Our children look from me to their father. They wrap their small arms around my neck and his legs in gestures of comfort. I wonder if they can imagine a time in the future when it will be their turn to mourn, when they will have to remember the water, the birdseed, the prayers.

The prayer ends, and we stand and smooth our clothes, blow our noses. As we gather our things, I pull a few last weeds from the voluminous sage planted behind her tombstone. We head down the hill in silence, reluctantly re-entering the mundane thoughts of the day. The children run ahead. They can recognize their family name in Arabic now, and they stop every so often in front of a tombstone to see if there is any relation buried there.

SAÏDA MANOUBIA

Although Tunisia is a Muslim country, a strong tradition of the cults of saints persists. Perhaps it harks back to tribal polytheism, or perhaps the saints offer a human face, comfort, and guidance, as they do in Christianity. While the mosque remains largely the domain of the men, the *marabou*, or tombs of the saints, offer the more feminine and colloquial face of spirituality. Here, mostly women - mothers and sisters, aunts and daughters - congregate to share their woes and appeal to their favourite saint. They come bearing offerings of incense, money, and lovingly prepared food. Before each shrine is a courtyard with a water source, a well reputed to have curative properties. Plastic water bottles are filled to overflowing, incantations and prayers offered before and after drinking or splashing the beneficent water over face and hands. It is not uncommon to see a group of women sitting on the ground in the courtyard, skirts fanned out over crossed legs, bare feet, talking about what brought them there, sharing news of one kind or another. They might be eating, or singing together, and sometimes a fight may break out. None of this is considered unusual or separate from the devotion that has brought them there, which goes on inside the shrine, undisturbed.

Consider Saïda Manoubia, patron saint of Tunis. Women come in droves, on Mondays or Fridays, asking her intercession in misfortunes ranging from sterility to an unhappy marriage. Offerings - *wa'ada* - of *couscous* and oil provide sustenance for the keeper of the shrine - the *zarda* - and those seeking refuge. Saïda Manoubia's shrine is a popular *rendez-vous* for star-crossed lovers and offers shelter for women seeking refuge from abusive husbands, tyrannical fathers, or overzealous brothers. The legend of Saïda Manoubia has come to represent the struggle of all women in traditional Tunisia, and she serves in memory as she did in life, as their special champion and protector. She is also, historically, the patron saint of all the oppressed, misunderstood, and discarded people of society. She is the iconic double legend of Tunis, where she lived, and Manouba, a small village on the outskirts, where she grew up. Her story reads like something from *A Thousand and One Nights*, and is told with more than one version.

Saïda Manoubia (translated as the saint from Manouba) was reputedly the only child, extraordinary and beautiful, of an older merchant and his wife. Already at a very young age, she showed an unusual proclivity for intellectual and spiritual pursuits, engaging in informed discussions with scholars even before puberty. One can only surmise how this might have come about, given the fact that she lived in the thirteenth century, when it was hardly conventional practice to teach daughters to read and write. Perhaps, as an only child, she had recourse to an education, or perhaps, as is often the case with young children, she played at her father's side in his workplace and conversed with the customers. I know from experience that a child exposed to adults in their work environment becomes adept at speaking their language and often finds their company more interesting than that of her own peers.

As she matured, her conversations, along with her developing beauty, drew attention. As an adolescent, she was supposed to be sequestered at home, awaiting her wedding day. Instead, she would wander the town with scholars and mosque officials, discussing matters of philosophy and faith. This was unheard of and caused her father great consternation. One day she went missing, and was found in deep discourse with a young man on the outskirts of town. They had wandered too far, distracted by their subject, and had found shelter under a shady tree. For her father, this was the last straw—being alone with a man was strictly forbidden. He took her home and immediately arranged a marriage with a distant cousin.

Here the legend forks into two versions. In one, she strikes her betrothed with a magic arrow on their wedding night, rendering him insane, then runs away. In the other, my favorite, she proposes to her father that she perform a miracle to prove her innocence in exchange for his forgiveness and her freedom. He agrees, and she bids him slaughter a steer, keep the head, and distribute the meat to friends and neighbors, instructing them to return the bones to him when they have finished. Once collected, she murmurs an incantation over the carcass and the animal is mystically, magically reassembled, a shining black steer with powerful horns, snorting and pawing the ground, whole and fully animated. Awestruck and humbled, her father lets her go, and she is free.

Released from the obligations of home and hearth, she sought out the most downtrodden and miserable places in which to live and do God's work - the fringe neighborhoods of Tunis' sprawling metropolis, places where only thieves and prostitutes dared to make their homes. She settled there and spun wool to earn her living. This is what makes her a hero; it's not just the fact that society's outcast were welcome in her home, that she fed and clothed them, healed their wounds and taught them, but that she labored as they did, lived among them, even though she didn't have to, even though she was a miracle worker.

She was not a saint in the way the Christians might think of a saint. She offered succor to thieves and those running from their debts, anyone unjustly persecuted or coerced. She gave to the poor, offering ten sheep during feast time to the father of a large family who could not afford even one. But there are other stories, mysterious and salacious. She lived mostly alone, sometimes with a male disciple. She increasingly spent her time in meditation on God's passion and making love, apparently as a kind of initiation. Ultimately, her entourage consisted almost entirely of men, and the ballads that tell her tale are mostly erotic in nature. Her saliva was said to have curative properties, as well as being capable of putting her patients into a state of drunken ecstasy.

Nonetheless, these attributes were described by her as nothing in comparison with God's love. She routinely mocked the officials and dignitaries who insisted upon seeking her audience, submitting them to legendary humiliations. She had no tolerance for the privileged class and, on one occasion, after having repeatedly refused to grant an audience to the Sultan, forced him to crawl to her on hands and knees when she finally gave him an appointment. As the neighborhoods she inhabited improved, due largely to her efforts, she moved further away, always seeking out the domain of the undesirables. Eventually, her life transformed into one of renunciation, asceticism, and complete harmony with nature.

Lalla Aicha (Saïda Manoubia)
By Ahmed Khudja, 18th c. Tunisian poet
(Translated from the French by Dorothea Biba Naouai)

Deep in my heart, a flame burns,
My soul is the hostage of its love for a woman
Life rips itself from the dying body
Sleep departs from weeping eyes!
Oh, you, the reason for my pain,
Aicha, beauty with the black eyes,
Aicha, Saint of the World.
Why are you so far away
Always far away.
Why, why, the Manoubian!

My ardent passions,
Love and desire,
Meet only with your cold indifference.
My love for you
Has left me beaten… humiliated…
Like a wilted plant.
Oh, beauty with the black eyes,
Oh, shady oak in the distant sky.

Rebel of my desires,
If you are irritated
I will bring you offerings.
Respond to my appeals
Oh eternal saint
You promised me words
In my dreams, in my slumber.

The miracles written
In your sacred book
Arrive in our hearts
And in our inflamed souls.

Purest gold you are,
As is everything you have loved.

The libertine approached you
Entreated you, touched you.

His parched desire
By your gentle will
Transformed into love
Of God and of piety.
To the devoted who wished
To chase away this miscreant
You said, "Pour him
The wine of lovers,
Of the beloved faithful,
Wine of love, of holiness."

This is not the language of the mosques. And yet, the ultimate intention is the same: worship God, treat each other with love and compassion. I think another reason Saïda Manoubia is beloved by women is because she embodies what so many women have pursued or fantasized about at one time or another since time immemorial: flouting the conventions of society and setting out on our own, exchanging husband, reputation, children, for the pursuit of our innermost convictions. Whether we hail from Tunis, New York City, or Bloomfield, New Jersey, doesn't this resonate with the women's marches across the country, the #metoo movement? Her story speaks of fantastic, epic qualities of feminine courage and generosity. No kowtowing to patriarchal authority or tradition, no hesitant insecurity. Instead, unconditional love for the downtrodden, devotion in action. I think of her and want to be more like her. She bespeaks a feminine power I dream of, and that I have seen peeking from behind the *sefseri* in Tunisia, covert and powerful.

TO KNOW A VEIL

In every color of the sherbet rainbow, they sashay down the Avenue Bourguiba. Matching outfits, from the embroidery that decorates the neckline and cuffs of the long kaftan shirts to the swishy, bellbottomed pants of a similar shade of linen, all coordinated perfectly with the gauzy scarf on top. Sunglasses and handbags, freshly picked from the latest fashion magazines, complete the ensemble. The veil is back in fashion!

The year is 2004, and post-9/11 has brought the Muslim world into a new discourse with faith and practice. In Tunisia which is economically and culturally so closely tied to Europe, the veil is making a comeback for the first time since before Tunisia's independence in the late fifties. Carelessly draped over the head and across the shoulders or meticulously folded, wrapped and then pinned so that no hair escapes, every young woman seems to be wearing one.

The *hijab*, or veil, is mentioned in the Koran as a means for women to exercise modesty in public. Its use has an extraordinarily complex and fascinating history, particularly in Tunisia.

As concerns this subject in the Koran, men are encouraged to lower their gaze and the women to "draw their veils over their bosoms and not display their beauty".

Islamic law and diverse traditions across the Muslim world have made for a great variety of interpretations. To different women at different times, the *hijab* has meant anything from a simple kerchief, covering only the hair, to the full body covering known as the *chador*, or *burkha*, which leaves only the opening of a screened slit for the eyes. Tunisia, which witnessed so many transformations as a country, has also been subject to myriad fluctuations of what it means to dress appropriately as a woman, especially during the past century.

A head covering is a necessity in a hot country, particularly one that borders on the Sahara desert; one has only to think of the nomadic Berber tribes, their layers of fabric and their turbans to protect against sun, wind, and sand. Or the many depictions of the Virgin Mary, whose home was Jerusalem. As such, scarves and shawls, for both men and women, were already part of the local dress vocabulary long before Islam arrived in the early eighth century. And Tunisia, the very definition of a melting pot, would have accepted and incorporated many different styles and interpretations once the veil became a necessary part of prescribed attire for Muslim women. Influences abound, from the Aghlabid and Fatimid dynasties, who came from the Middle East towards the end of the first millennium; to the flamboyant Spanish and Portuguese refugees, who settled here during the Middle Ages; to the Ottoman Turks, with their refined opulence, who ruled from the mid-15th century until Tunisia was colonized by the French in the late 19th century. All came and left their mark; in the architecture, the cuisine, the decoration of ceramics, in the music and, perhaps most prominently, in the way the women covered themselves.

During my mother-in-law's youth and the time of the French occupation, the veil as an indicator of class. Prostitutes, for example, were forbidden to wear them. Nana, on the other hand, as the daughter of a *checheiya* merchant, the most established and highly regarded of all trades, wore a *chador*, covering herself completely, signaling to the outside world her status. In much the same way, only the most prestigious houses had a *gueneria*, a wooden-screened bay window on the second story, from which the ladies of the house could observe the comings and goings of the neighbors in the street below without themselves being seen. Girls and women were traditionally kept at home, the outside world of men considered a dangerous labyrinth of menace and seduction. For these women, the veil was not considered a symbol of oppression, but instead a form of protection, a sign of the degree to which a woman was valued in her family and, by extension, the degree to which she valued herself. Moreover, as Nana replied when I asked her about her reasons for wearing the *chador*, it was fashionable at the time - *moda*!

When Habib Bourguiba, champion of Tunisian independence from French rule, was released from French prison as the first leader of the new Tunisian Republic, everything changed. It was 1956. Bourguiba was anxious to establish Tunisia as a modern country, free and independent as defined by the West. He quickly established a government with many modern reforms, including new emancipation laws for women. Among these was the abolition of the veil. It was now illegal for a woman to wear the veil in any public place: hospitals, government offices, universities, schools. Obviously, this reform met with much controversy. For all but the most adventurous, going beyond the confines of home without a veil was tantamount to exposing oneself in public. Bourguiba, in his desire to emancipate the Tunisian woman, was asking her to choose between her traditions and the law. The veil, touted by colonialists in Muslim countries around the world as evidence of oppressive treatment of women, had become loaded with meaning far beyond the Koran's simple call to modesty for Europeans and Muslims alike.

But Tunisians are used to juggling tradition against the whims of the current authority. The women of my husband's generation, growing up in the sixties and seventies in newly liberated Tunisia, were getting one message in school and another at home. Public school was available to girls and boys alike and taught in Arabic for the first time in decades, but the upper classes were still sending their children to the French Catholic schools that remained and were considered superior in quality. In either case, veiling was forbidden. Later, they took jobs, and learned to copy European dress from magazines and the movies shown on recently acquired television sets. They learned to bare ankles and forearms, as well as their luxurious, seductive hair, without shame, much to the anxiety and concern of their parents. "We are liberated!" they protested. "What's liberating about being naked?" asked their mothers in response. That generation produced scores of women who would not wear the veil except in certain places – the Mosque, the cemetery, their wedding ceremonies – who, bilingual and armed with doctorates, nonetheless often stayed home to care for their families once they were married.

When I first started coming to Tunisia, the women of my mother-in-law's generation didn't go out unless they had at least a headscarf to cover their hair. Most wore, and many still wear, the white *sefseri* over their clothing and scarf. This garment, a standard part of every Tunisian woman's *trousseau* even today, is simply a large, ivory damask rectangle. It is drawn over the crown of the head and shoulders and loosely wrapped around the body, much like the Indian *sari*. Crossed over the bosom, it is then tucked into a string tied under the breasts expressly for this purpose. If no string is available, it is anchored by the arm-pits and casually held together in front by the teeth. One of our adult nephews remembers going to the market and seeing the *sefseri*-clad women, like flocks of birds or angels, weaving in and out among the brightly colored fruits and vegetables. I, myself, covet the *sefseri* and secretly harbor a fantasy of wrapping myself up like a delicate pastry to run errands.

Back to *nos jours*, the beginning of the second millennium: For two years now, I have noticed a sudden increase in the ap-pearance of the *hijab*. Young women of every social stratus, un-married, married, educated or working class, rich or poor, are amassing collections of the veil as the most important current accessory. Seen in the context of shifting international percep-tions of Muslims and the Arab world, or the uprisings and recent legislation in France concerning a woman's right to wear the veil in public, one might assume that this recent phenomenon re-flects a sentiment of solidarity. We are Muslims, these women are saying, and we are not what you think. Indeed, countless ar-ticles and documentaries in recent years have debated just that. Without a doubt, many women, at least those living in countries with secular rule, like Tunisia or Turkey or France, have made a conscious choice to return to tradition, to establish their identity as faithful Muslims. In many cases, the reappearance of the veil is part of a worldwide renewal of religious observance. Having gorged on the fruits of industry and capitalism, many people of all faiths and in all countries find themselves on a spiritual quest, seeking to bring order and meaning to their lives.

For a fair number of Tunisian women, though, my unveiled friends and relations whisper, the veil is worn to attract a good husband, someone in good standing, with an education and from a good family, hopefully providing a step up on the socio-eco-nomic ladder for the young woman. Even today, a potential wife is prized for her modesty and her piety, particularly in established traditional families for whom clear hereditary lineage and the correct upbringing of the children is of primary importance. Some lament this phenomenon as part of a wave of modern hypocrisy in which men enjoy their whisky during the week and then spend Fridays in the mosque exhibiting their piety.

As I watch them, the thought occurs to me that many of these women might simply be enjoying the textures and colors of the gauzy fabrics, the way the veil flutters out behind them, the elements of fashion and rebellion, doing the opposite of what their mothers did. They know that their beauty is not in the least diminished by the veiling but enhanced by it, made less accessible and thereby infinitely more desirable. Many of them obviously delight in the sweetly seductive quality this new modesty offers. Most of the young women in Tunisia with whom I speak are not defined by the veil. They have chosen it for their own reasons. They will study and work and raise families and practice their faith without relinquishing one iota of their femininity. All of this in a country where the veil is still illegal in public spaces, where, in light of the current political climate, veil raids are periodically performed in schools and students expelled who refuse to comply. I ask my nieces what happens when these women have to go to school or to work. They tell me that the veils get tucked surreptitiously into handbags or tied around the handles of the market basket. In the same way, during the French occupation, Tunisian children, who were not allowed to speak Arabic in school, would speak it as soon as they were out of earshot of their teachers.

In any case, my nieces, most of them unveiled, dismiss the whole phenomenon as *moda*, fashion, just as their grandmother did. One of them, when asked if she will wear the veil, replies that she hasn't ruled it out, but that she wants to be sure she'd be doing it for the right reasons. "After all," she says, "most of them are riding on the backs of their boyfriends' motorcycles, wearing tight jeans, or sitting with them in cafés, definitely *haram*!"

The year is 2017. Much time has passed. We have lived through the euphoric hope of the Arab Spring, ignited by Tunisia, and the dark turbulence in its wake. As Tunisia struggles to establish a new identity, political, economic, and social instability have become the norm. Brutal killings of tourists in the Bardo museum and on a popular beach in Sousse have enhanced, in the eyes of the international community, a troubling association with Islamic extremism. On the one hand, the Tunisian police investigate conservative Muslims. Cars carrying bearded men and women wearing the *chador* are stopped routinely at increasingly prolific roadblocks. They are questioned intensely, their trunks searched for weapons. On the other hand, the women who do not wear the veil leave the house in constant fear of assault by conservative Muslims. In France, Muslim women who cover themselves at the beach are harassed and even arrested, while I wonder if it is safe to let my youngest daughter, now sixteen, wear her bikini at our beach in Soliman.

Amidst all of this unrest in Tunisia, one evening, at home in Bloomfield, NJ, I have the following experience: My mother, who is now nearly 80, was born in Berlin during the war and experienced separation from her family during evacuation, and the arduous rebuilding of Germany and the deep shame of her country's history. A semi-retired violin teacher, she has, in recent years, devoted more of her time and resources to her meditation practice. After a number of retreats – in Vermont, Connecticut, Peru, India - she is now cleaning out her closets and deciding what to keep and what to give away. During a retreat in India participants were asked to bring a few special accessories for use during the meditation sessions. One of them she now offers to me. Folded up in her arms, it appears to be a large pale blue cloth. I have not seen it before, and she now asks me if I would like to have it, as I am the only one she knows who might even understand where it's from.

I have received a number of gifts from people who have said similar things - this is supposed to be Tunisian, you will surely like it/know what is is/know what to do with it. My German grandmother once bequeathed me a voluminous, woolen men's hooded cape with black embroidery embellishments that she had acquired on a long-ago senior tour of Tunisia. She also gave me an appliquéed embroidery piece she herself had made; a camel train with turbaned drivers, each face a slightly different shade of brown.

So, I take the garment from my mother and notice first its color, a crisp light blue, so light as to be almost white. Like fresh snow on a clear, sunny day. Then I notice its weight; heavy, finely pleated material and lots of it. Fine linen, perhaps, or viscose, rayon? As I turn it in my hands, I notice embroidery around a screened face panel - my mother is giving me a *chador*! My liberated, German-Berkeley hippie-child-free-spirit-bohemian mother has little notion of what this means, how heavy this garment she's offering. I feel acutely flooded with history, the history of my husband's country, his faith traditions, the current conversation in the world. She tells me the disciples of the Indian guru with whom she was studying, male and female, were asked to bring a white garment that would cover the entire body, including the head and face, to protect against malevolent spirits during meditation.

I am curious. I have lived and talked with enough women in Tunisia to understand that the conversation around the veil is not so simple, and I have been on the outside of that conversation, looking in. I own a *sefseri* but have yet to muster the courage to wear it in public, in Tunisia or elsewhere. Suddenly, I have this urge to try on the *chador*. In my little Bloomfield, NJ kitchen, mother beaming, I wade through the heavy fabric to find its opening and draw it over my head. It takes some pulling and adjusting to get it fitted correctly so that I can see through the small, screened panel. I draw the voluminous ends around me so that nothing is showing but the toes of my grey woolen house slippers. My perception of the light changes, filtered through the pale blue cloth. I take a breath. Peace. Quiet. No fear. And yes, an undeniable sense of safety, of protection; from the hungry gazes of people, from their conversation, from any interaction I might wish to avoid. The feeling is one of complete and utter privacy. I can see you, but you need my permission if you want to see me. I have the power to let you in or keep you out. I think of the tents I used to make as a child: sheets draped over the chairs I arranged in a circle. Stuffed animals and pets in, sister and parents out. The same serene feeling of gently filtered light. The same feeling of solace. I think of the insecurity, the awkward exposure I have often felt in public. This would have been an amazing thing to have in middle school!

I wonder at my response. Clearly, I am not making a life-changing decision to wear this garment in the streets of NYC or Bloomfield. When I share the experience with my now seventeen-year-old daughter and invite her to try on the *chador*, her response is immediate, and unequivocal: "No, mama. That's creepy.". Her romantic relationship with a young woman would not be accepted in Tunisia, not today, not ten years ago, nor any time before that. During the revolution, one of the hopeful slogans we saw spray-painted on walls was "Tunisia is not a homophobic country," yet we know those who live their love in secret still.

I suppose, in the end, the deciding factor of what makes wearing the *hijab*, the *burkha*, or the *chador* an act of modesty, an act of liberation, an act of faith, or an act of oppression, is determined by two things: choice and intention. Who has decided to wear it? Or who has decided it must be worn. And what is the desire, deep in the heart of the woman who covers herself with the veil? Is she under orders from her father? Or is she trying to placate her brother? Please her husband? Is she playing a socio-political card for safety? Does she have a deep and abiding sense of faith which leads her to keep her femininity protected because of her relationship with God? Is she truly modest, shy, self-conscious, like so many women from every country, every culture, every walk of life, and does the veil serve as her oasis, her refuge? Or is it, as Zeinib ben Saad Naouai, our dearly departed Nana, once said: *moda*!

MOSAÏC

The garden walls of our home look so white and the days are long. No TV, no internet. The scratchy radio plays 'Mosaic FM,' a station that alternates between the distinctive sounds of traditional Tunisian, Egyptian or Lebanese ballads, and the sleek commercial beat of Europe's finest (Stromae) or American artists like Justin Timberlake. It occurs to me that we might create a mosaic on the northern wall. Impassioned family discussion ensues and finally we all agree that it should be a fish. It's a simple enough shape for beginners such as ourselves, and we can use pieces of broken tile left over from the work on our bathroom, as well as the bits we find in the sand from construction rubble during our walks to the beach. In a matter of days, we have amassed a good collection of tile pieces and drawn several sketches of fish. The project has galvanized us all and no one is bored any longer. Ali buys some cement and grout, and pretty soon we are all involved in making the fish mosaic on the garden wall. Myriad shades of aquamarine, indigo, and true Tunisian blue negotiate for space in the hand-drawn outline of the large-finned, full-lipped fish.

A lonely ochre chip is set aside for the eye, and within a couple of days' work, our fish is ready for grouting. Ali applies the grout with care, then wipes it down, buffs it with a clean cloth. It is totally brilliant. We are so proud.

Mosaics are part of a well-established artisanal tradition of ceramics in Tunisia, carried over from her Roman days as Carthage. You can purchase small mosaics in the *souk* - an eye, a hand of Fatima, a fish - as souvenirs. These are newer creations, but there is a wealth of mosaics dating from Roman times still available for viewing at the Musée Bardo in Tunis. As a family, we have made the pilgrimage to the Musée Bardo a yearly tradition. The museum houses an outstanding collection of these ancient mosaics, artfully displayed in what used to be a *bey*'s palace. Fabulous Ottoman ceilings painted gold and turquoise alternate with expansive, light-filled, pillared courtyards, creating a respite from the hot and crowded city. The children were always glad for the outing, the cool and spacious interior. They scurry around surreptitiously, avoiding the stern gaze of the security guards.

The mosaics themselves are precious testaments to classical Mediterranean life. Dolphins frolic among swimmers in the gently curling waves of the deep blue sea, a shepherd with a pipe sits peacefully in a field of wheat. Floating across the background of ivory-hued tesserae, a domestic still life depicts a terra cotta carafe and a bowl of green-leafed olives, while doves and other fowl parade ceremoniously. Harmony and a deep love of the everyday pervade these marble tapestries, some of which cover entire floors, span entire walls.

The Tunisian tesserae are prized above all for their color: richly-hued burgundies, emerald greens, deep slate blues, and mustard golds. I learn this from a well-heeled antiquities dealer, years after our first visit to the Bardo, on a cold winter's day in a gallery on Madison Avenue in NYC. The style is clearly Roman, but the bombastic themes of the Roman empire are replaced with something much softer, more domestic and inviting. One imagines a very patient, selective artisan, contemplating his work as he places the tiny squares, one at a time, watching the picture emerge, focusing all his efforts on one small area for hours. I come as much to bask in this atmosphere of peaceful craft in in celebration of ordinary life as to educate my children. In a city where much is dilapidated, the Musée Bardo is a jewel, well preserved and lovingly cared for.

Flash forward several years after that first mosaic in our garden, and then a second, a larger hand of Fatima on the western wall. The children are nearly grown and it's been years since we last went as a family. After we sold the restaurant, finances were tight, and the kids became increasingly involved in summer activities that kept them in Bloomfield with their friends. Tunisia was initially destabilized by the revolution in 2011, reeling from numerous and often conflicting efforts to establish a government in line with the wishes of the people. It seemed chaotic but benign from our home in the US. Elections followed the revolution, then protests erupted again when the new government fell short of expectations. After these protests, more elections followed and, finally, a new constitution. We keep track of the developments on French TV5, the magazine *Jeune Afrique*, and reports from Tunis via Facebook and telephone. Friends and relatives in Tunis are cynical, reporting mostly on how trash collection has become unmanageable, how lines at municipal offices have doubled, how prices of ordinary items keep going up. Nothing will change, many of them say. We should have left well enough alone. We are unfit for democracy. We need a strong hand to keep the chaos at bay.

Then, on March 18th, 2015, we hear the report of twenty-one tourists killed by 3 terrorists at the Musée Bardo. It's all over the news. We are shocked. Tunisia's greatest fear has been confirmed. And the western world's, too - wasn't Tunisia the Muslim country that offered an example of temperance and societal evolution? In our own family, we joined those who lauded Tunisia for reminding us of how democracy works, what ordinary citizens are capable of. Before the revolution, when people asked Ali where he was from, the answer would provoke a quizzical frown. After the Arab Spring, they saw Tunisia with respect, even admiration. She led the way for other revolutions and protests - Egypt, Syria, Occupy Wall Street - though none as successful as her own and some with far-reaching and disastrous consequences.

The perpetrators can't be Tunisian, we think, and yet they are, as it turns out. As it turns out, many hundreds of young people have left Tunisia for Libya, Syria, Iraq to join the extremists and fight for their cause. The Tunisians we know are hot-tempered, we tell ourselves, but not violent in that way. They don't kill in cold blood. Radical Islam has been kept at bay, snuffed out in our beloved country, or so we thought. Tunisia has historically been a haven for the moderate Muslim. Go to the mosque or don't, wear the *hijab* or don't, drink your glass of wine at home, it's no one's business but your own and God's.

And then another attack follows in late June at a resort in Sousse, just about an hour from our home. This one is even worse, even more violent; more carnage, thirty-eight dead. The perpetrator, again, Tunisian. I am given the news by my colleagues, nurses at the hospital in New Jersey where I work with newborn babies and their mothers. Our small unit serves largely new immigrant populations: Chinese, Egyptian, Brazilian, Palestinian, Ukrainian, Syrian, Mexican, Haitian. We are a study in culturally appropriate patient care. My co-workers are concerned for me because, as they know, we have booked tickets for Tunisia and are scheduled to leave the following week. We are going as a family, for the first time in seven years. My stepdaughters will fly in from Montreal, the older one with the baby, our first grandchild.

All of this information spins in my mind. Let me check in with my husband, my children. One by one they offer their unanimous resolve: we go to Tunisia. After all, they argue, what about the recent attack on a Bible study group in Charleston, South Carolina? Fanatics are everywhere, killing innocent people in the name of what? Our youngest daughter, Aicha, a freshman in high school now, explains to her history teacher that she feels safer going to Tunisia than she does traveling within her own country. Guns are harder to come by over there.

So we go, all of us together and without fear. But we stay clear of the Musée Bardo, as well as other tourist hot spots, all of them hemorrhaging seasonal revenue now. They offer discounted admission and hotel packages at the eleventh hour, filling up with Tunisians who've never before been able to afford a resort vacation and with Algerians, curious and lured over the border by the cheaper prices. There is a feeling of heightened alert in the pervasive police presence, but also of life as usual in the popular neighborhoods. There are fewer European goods available, and what is available is more expensive. Infrastructure has been negatively affected as increasingly scarce government funds are re-allocated to security. Trash collection, petty municipal bureaucracies, the postal service, all instantly feel the sting to their budgets. Special forces, looking very sharp in black uniforms, stand guard at prominent intersections leading to the beaches. They signal any cars that carry bearded men or veiled women, asking them to pull over. The police will inspect their papers for validity and search their cars.

I suppose this makes everyone feel more secure, but how effective can this process of screening be for what we already know, when someone who really wants to do damage will come from an unexpected place, in an unexpected way? The terrorist who shot indiscriminately into the crowded beach looked like any modern young Tunisian man: beardless, with curly hair slightly longer than conventionally accepted, stylish sunglasses – Ray-bans, maybe, or Vuarnet.

In the face of terrorism of any kind, faith in a greater creative force paradoxically offers solace to the victims' families and potential targets, while also giving courage to the attackers. I have heard Ali say so many times in response to my well-honed existential fears: "When it's your time to go, it's your time to go, no matter where you are, or how you've prepared." Can I find some comfort in this wisdom, and in the meditation practice that reminds me again and again to favor the present moment's bounty over the myriad possible narratives of past and future?

Maybe, but, my northern European mind wants an explanation, wants closure regarding what I see as a paradox between the peace-loving day-to-day activities of the Mediterranean soul and the devastating violence of the attackers in Bardo and Sousse. Who are these people? How can they be Tunisian? Sons and brothers and fathers, just like the people I know. Are we entering a new era of destruction in the country of my children's ancestors?

For clues, I go back to Tunisia's earlier history, before Tunis was Carthage, back to when it was ruled by the Phoenicians, rulers of the Mediterranean and masters of trade. Chapter after chapter of the guide book I consult reveals bloody battles, surreptitious take-overs, corrupt and ineffectual ruling parties, insouciant wheeling and dealing with the de-facto agents of power. Again and again, the poor and powerless are bought and sold, coerced or manipulated into supplying goods and services or political support in favor of the chosen ruler. The Phoenicians are conquered by the Romans, who, in turn are destroyed by the

Vandals. The Vandals are overcome by the Arabs, and the Arabs yield to the Turks. The Turks finally succumb to the French, and the French, after seventy-plus years in power, set Tunisia free while maintaining parasitical trade and commerce relationships. At any given time during these occupations and transfers of power, there are clandestine groups preparing to destabilize and overthrow the ruling party. Secret allegiances are made, long-standing relationships severed. Tunisian history is rife with betrayal, pirates, guerilla warriors and assassins. Because of its strategic location and its indelible identity as a mercantile society, circuitous deals are made with each transfer of power so that business can go on as usual. It sounds so familiar...

In fact, as I enter more deeply into discussion with my husband and oldest son, now nineteen, they remind me of Europe's own past, and America's; the Spanish Inquisition, colonialism, the Holocaust, the mass destruction of Native Americans, slavery and the lynching of black men, the Civil Rights movement and police brutality which continues today, and the increasing inequities here and elsewhere of the one versus the ninety-nine percent. Corruption and greed happen in the highest levels of corporations and in every government in every country including, especially it seems, our own United States. And yet countries and communities and families have patched together their lives, one meal at a time, moment by moment, making each day a mosaic of intimate events of many colors and flavors.

So there is nothing incongruous, I come to realize, about the tranquil domesticity of the mosaics at the Musée Bardo and the terrorist attackers of the tourists who came to view them. Nothing paradoxical about the presence of the black-clad special forces and the complacency of the locals shopping for supper ingredients in the open market. Tunisians have been doing what they do for generations regardless of the forces that circle and menace. Like so many of the world's poor and working class-es, they understand that political change is rarely steady and straightforward, politicians rarely familiar with the lives of their constituents. Since the attack in the Bardo and the one in Sousse, three nieces have married, two babies have been born in our family. Life goes on.

At the house in Soliman, the mosaics remain a souvenir of our family's youth. The hand seems to be missing some grout in places. We had finished it the night before our return flight, many years ago, and entrusted a neighbor to the grouting and polishing. My husband's touch is wanted but he assures us he will repair and polish it so that it looks as beautiful as the fish mosaic. In the center of the hand, we had left a space in the shape of a heart. We have not yet found the material to fill it. Red tile is rare, and Ali suggests filling the space with a piece of mirror, so that when you look at the hand of Fatima, you see in its center your own image. Time will give us the solution. Just as time will support the growth of the tree that now hides the fish mosaic on the north wall. One day, its lowest branches will have grown high above the wall and the mosaic will be visible again. The tree was an opportunist, a vagrant seed blown from who knows where. But its thin green leaves are abundant and its shade will be a welcome place to put a reading chair or two.

IMMOLATION

I have witnessed firsthand the self-inflicted acts of desperation. A fresh scar, a jagged purple welt on a smooth olive-skinned cheek, rendering indelible that fight with the oppressive, arrogant spouse; the ungrateful, wayward son; the impassive boss. After so much supplication, negotiation, adaptation, taking the heat, circumventing the tyranny, the impervious dropping of a final straw. And then the hand reaches up and tears through the flesh of its own face, its own beautiful skin, in an effort to keep from directing the violence outward, so as to minimize collateral damage, to leave no regrets to compound the pain. Among the few outlets available to those who struggle materially are work, love, TV, sleep, fighting, or the shallow inebriation offered by Celtia beer, watered down, consumed in private and laced with shame.

So, on December 17, 2010, when Mohammed Bouazzizi set himself on fire, I thought of family members and friends and the persistent churn of frustration in Tunisia. How many times had Mohammed Bouazzizi organized his day, gone to market late at night, woke up early in the morning, leaving his mother's home where his sisters slept? He was saving to educate his sisters, to buy a pickup truck so that he could leave the cumbersome hand truck behind and, once gas and repairs were paid, maybe even make an extra buck for himself. He wanted to get married and have a family of his own someday. After all, he was a young man of twenty-six. Since his father had passed away, his meager income and what his mother earned working in the fields was all they had to live on, with little left over to finance his dreams. The permit to sell fruits in the market was an expense he couldn't assume. Better to take a chance that the policemen would accept the bribe of ten dinars and maybe a bag of fruit and then let him be—until the next time.

How many times had he gone without, worked extra hours, in the bright hope of raising his family above the level of poverty, ushering them into the twenty-first century with smart phones and electric washing machines? How many times had he taken the freshly pressed jeans from his mother's hands, and felt, with increasing apprehension, her confidence in him, her encouragement? How many times had the policemen checking for permits taken the bribes, the peaches and pears, all the while making him feel he was on shaky ground, vulnerable, powerless? The policemen themselves likely suffered from the pressure of their superiors, their government, that paid them barely enough to subsist on, yet expected them to keep their citizens in line. All across post-colonial Africa, the question of power is the most important one. Who are you afraid of?

No wonder then, that on that winter morning, having set his mind and heart to the hard labor before him, having suffocated frustration and dejectedness again and again, he had reached the limits of his capacity to submit to humiliation and defeat and had lost it completely. Lost his good sense, lost his composure, "snapped a cable".

Perhaps, on that day, he'd overslept. Some days things tumble against and into each other in a perfect storm. Maybe he had missed his breakfast or, asking his mother to make more, she had reprimanded him for sleeping late, revealing the frustration and disappointment that she, too, had been battling. Had she lost hope, finally, that her son would succeed in bringing her out of the hand-to-mouth life that had worn her down all these years? Perhaps, then, empty-bellied, he had arrived late to pick up his produce, the best fruits already gone. Then, still late, hurried on to the market where, like any ecosystem where competition for limited resources is fierce, the early bird gets the best spot for his fruit cart, closest to the coveted places in the covered market, where the wealthier merchants have their secured spots.

And then, having finally set everything up on the perimeter of the market, firm in his resolve to redeem the day with charm and extra effort to offset the disadvantages he had suffered, *In-ch'Allah* he would bring home some hard-earned cash, fifty *dinars* at least. He would have to sell his fruit for a bit less since some were bruised. But he knew how to arrange them in a high pyramid so that they looked like the best of the crop.

And then, on top of all that, the insult of the dreaded police officer coming to check for his permit to sell. It's a woman officer this time, and she is adamant in her refusal to accept the bribe. I imagine he turns on the charm, tries to gain her sympathy, maybe even flirts with her a little. But she will have none of it. Why not? Is she new to the job, or does her husband provide a second income, thereby making her immune to the bribe? Maybe it's just her personality, generally or on that particular day, unyielding. Is there personal history between them? It is a small town, after all. Were they high school students together? Were there feelings between them perhaps, before one advanced to a slightly higher position in their shared society?

What happens then? Does Bouazzizi say something in a way that suggests disrespect? Or does she provoke him to escalate? So much is communicated with the eyes, gestures, inflection. Reputedly, she insults his deceased father and finally slaps his face, both ultimate and unforgiveable humiliations for a young man, especially coming from a woman in uniform. The fruit cart is confiscated. Perhaps his precious inventory is destroyed. Bouazzizi goes to the municipal office to complain, but they refuse to grant him audience. Perhaps they tell him dispassionately that they are on their coffee break, the prerogative of bureaucracies all over the world. He leaves and, upon returning, sets himself on fire in front of the building, the spark that takes his life and ignites the Arab Spring.

What was going through his mind, I wonder, in the hours before he doused himself with fuel and lit the match? Did the heat of his shame and fury abate at any moment to let in a shadow of doubt or fear? Did he notice even fleetingly that he was hungry, or think with regret of his mother and sisters? Or was he calm, having finally formulated a plan, thinking that this his next act was the one good thing, a creative act, liberation? Could he have envisioned, just before the flames became all-consuming, that millions would gather in his name, that his final act would inspire a beginning? The death of Mohammed Bouazzizi ignited a revolution that had been building for centuries, from decades of oppression, first by foreign powers, then by native rulers, themselves shaped by foreign powers. And its effects have reverberated throughout the world, setting a conversation in motion that cannot be silenced.

The citizens of Tunisia, educated, tuned in and aware of the world at large via the internet and European television, had had enough. For weeks, months afterward, Facebook became a vehicle of dissent, of political and artistic expression, and of encouragement from relatives abroad. Rappers' videos circulated alongside footage of the protesters being beaten, only to return in greater numbers, the storming of the Palais de Justice and the mansions of the wealthy government officials once President Ben Ali had fled the country. His decades-long corrupt government had seriously underestimated the power of its people. How could they expect their citizens to sit quietly as they amassed real estate and trade deals and all manner of material excess while many of the citizens struggled for bread and olives? Unlimited access to European television and American movies helped stimulate their appetites for a better life. Cousins and sisters returned from abroad to share and sometimes flaunt the wealth that seemed to drop from the trees in distant lands. The Tunisian capacity for hard work yielded the desired results in places far from home. The smart and fortunate left their native soil or became intensely religious, allying themselves with the mosques that offered material support and comfort. Or they became card players, petty thieves, alcoholics - no small accomplishment in a Muslim country.

By the year 2000, when my nephews were all entering their teenage years, each had one sole ambition: to leave Tunisia, to follow in the footsteps of their uncles. Of the five of them, three managed to immigrate. Two came to the US on student visas and one went to Dubai as a pastry chef. Their attempts yielded mixed results, unprepared as they were for the material seduction and financial burdens of life in America. But that was before 9/11. In my husband's generation, all the brothers had left, only the sisters remaining. Even educated, the women have historically married and had children by their mid-twenties, and any dreams of travel replaced by schedules and dinner menus and mothers-in-law.

Since the revolution, much has happened, but little has

changed. Progress comes in tiny steps, two forward, one back, and none of it linear, especially in Tunisia, where even the line for the post office teller looks like a huddle. After having "won" the elections for twenty consecutive years with "ninety-five percent" of the vote, Ben Ali, from exile, must have been astonished that hundreds of candidates presented themselves to run for office. He must have wondered when, after two years of bumbling around without producing the promised new constitution, the people again took to the streets and overthrew the government they themselves had elected - NOT GOOD ENOUGH!!!

With the present government and a new, secular constitution in place, Tunisia has taken a baby step forward. But there is much work to be done; European industry, which provided countless jobs, has all but disappeared from Tunisia, and there is no money for infrastructure. The Japanese have supplied new trains from Korea, but garbage is everywhere - in the streets, hanging from trees, rotting under bridges. Women's rights have been affirmed in law, but many are wearing the *hijab* again for fear that the *salafists*, extremists, will attack them otherwise. Freedom of expression and freedom of the press seem to be afflicted by similar insecurities, though it is certainly better than it was.

The biggest obstacle still appears to be the continued and increasing rates of unemployment, for the youth especially, educated or not. The festering sense of resignation makes the fight against corruption and violence a constant struggle. Nothing will ever change, I hear my Tunisian friends say, any effort is futile, "we are more pathetic than toads." "*Hakeka!* That's the way how it is..." And, yet, nearly ten years later, on the other side of the ocean, a man name George Floyd is killed by police in Minneapolis, over a supposedly counterfeit twenty-dollar bill, and the world erupts.

JOURNAL TIDBITS

Great word for thunder: *RRRRAAD!*

Snapshots:
Impressive, adult ram with formidable, curly-Q horns, tied to the awning of a *mischoui* stand, straining at the bit, the smoke of the grilled lamb wafting up through the air.

4 guys laughing and pushing a car in the blazing sun, down the highway to the next gas station.

People waiting for the morning commuter bus in a single line, making themselves thin to fit within the narrow shade cast by a tall palm tree.

A cafe in a courtyard with only two trees and all the tables gathered together in the shade.

Four six-week old kittens, black and grey-striped, playing in a plastic crate of wilted parsley.

A taxi driver gingerly, patiently navigating the swiss cheese road of potholes.

Impromptu house built of cardboard and chicken wire and

other found materials. Wall made of rocks and pieces of concrete. Sheep and a rooster roam freely. Water is borrowed from neighbors.

A sixty-year old man walks, two hours each way, from his home to the city where he sells *mischmoum* made of jasmine blossoms. He walks to save the train fare.

Vegetable vendor with an ultra-thin, deep red chili pepper tucked behind his ear, in the same way you see *mischmoum* or cigarettes or pencil stubs.

Louage (taxi-bus) from Tunis, hanging from the rear-view mirror: a dusty, desiccated fishtail; a medallion with verse from the Koran; a broken CD of the Koran; a pine-shaped air freshener. The driver stops frequently between official stops to greet friends, and to pass on the daily newspaper.

Here are some surprising things you will see in Tunisia:

Unfinished houses with people living in them.

Faces, scarred by fire or an unfortunate encounter with a knife, that have not been surgically "corrected."

Toes and toenails eaten by fungus, rendered unrecognizable, even in younger adults.

Dirty buckets filled with calf entrails being wheeled to market in the open sun, uncovered, visited by flies and unabashed dust.

Stray cats, pregnant, with matted fur and an ear or a tail lost to battle, stealing, with great calculation and finesse, a fresh sardine from a fishmonger's box at the market.

Festering sores on healthy children.

Garbage, loose and in open piles, strategically dumped in the street.

Human shit, floating alongside bathers in the open sea.

Eggs for sale, unrefrigerated, on a shelf in an un-airconditioned store, with stacked cages of chickens, barely alive and panting in the heat.

An entire calf's head, tongue lolling, suspended on a hook, to draw you into the butcher's stall.

Stray cows and dogs wandering the beach, or the streets looking for garbage. Ingesting, not infrequently, a plastic bag or two.

Babies eating sweets.

People without teeth, or with terrible teeth, laughing, smiling unabashedly, generously, infectiously.

Friends, no matter the age, holding hands. Friends and colleagues leaning on each other while reading the newspaper, or waiting for the bus, or just because.

Strangers kissing children in the middle of the street. Just because.

Strangers sharing water bottles, wiping the mouth of the bottle and uttering a '*bismillah*' for protection.

Old people, deranged people, physically disabled people, being cared for by their families, their neighbors.

Samples of cakes or fruit given to taste, as a marketing strategy, but infinitely more for the pleasant human exchange.

Plastic bottles reused and reused and reused for multiple purposes, filled with water to wash sand off the feet, to clean the tombstone or the car, filled with liquid soap or olive oil or *z'har* (orange blossom water), which can all be purchased in bulk from huge vats at the market.

AND....there is no dancing in public here, despite hours of rousing music on the beach; and no making out in public. Flirtation is a devastatingly subtle and astute practice. The young women are ravishing in their clinging-wet coverups. And the young men are dashing as only a Mediterranean stud can be, with oiled curls, bounding out of the sea to dive onto the sand after a soccer ball. They seduce each other with their eyes and their gestures, without ever touching. Lord only knows what goes on at night!

Not to forget, either, the smells: Passing by a café with its doors and windows open, you smell coffee mixed with the smells of tobacco, soap and water, perspiration, dust; riding in a car with the windows rolled down to move the air, you smell diesel exhaust, manure, rotisserie chickens, sunbaked dust, baking bread.

SOLIMAN PLAGE

I love my village. But there are those who complain. The streets remain unpaved despite promises from the municipality. Because of this, dust enters the houses, coughed up by the cars that rumble by. Garbage collection is a primitive affair. Sometime between eight-thirty and ten o'clock in the morning, a tractor rumbles past, announcing its arrival, and everyone rushes to take out the previous day's accumulation. Two men in blue smocks and straw hats collect the bags and toss them onto a flatbed that just manages to stay upright behind the tractor. Those who have invested in sturdy plastic garbage bins wait jealously to retrieve them and bring them back within the protection of their gated gardens. Those, like me, who have made the mistake of bringing the garbage out before the arrival of the tractor quickly learn that the receptacle, a coveted luxury item, risks disappearing. Or, in the absence of a garbage can, the garbage bag might be torn apart by hungry cows. These cows, of a breed unknown to me, are brown or white, or a soft grey with black markings. They bear no signs of ownership and wander freely in search of food, finding little in the dried-out fields of summer. The resulting jumble of milk cartons and carrot peels, coffee grounds and plastic bags, is shunned by the garbage collectors, and the citizen is left to retrieve it all with a shovel, and save it for the following day's tractor.

The same tractors drop groups of young men along the beach, armed with plastic bags and nothing with which to retrieve the garbage save their ungloved hands. Plastic water bottles, ice cream wrappers, oil-stained sandwich papers, loaded diapers, and the like are all collected in this manner. Because it is already ninety-five degrees, and because the task is unpleasant, the men make quick work of it, leaving much behind. The garbage cans that had originally been set out on the beach to facilitate collection, halved oil drums painted bright blue, have been removed for personal use over the years. They now serve as cement mixing receptacles, private garbage cans, planters, and multipurpose storage. The infrastructure exists, even for recycling, but the government workers are underpaid, and the people have resigned themselves to a certain degree of chaos amidst negligence and corruption.

One year, after many complaints from the citizens about the plastic problem, the town launched a well-publicized clean-up campaign. Children were encouraged to bring all of their plastic to the beach, with the heaviest bag winning a prize of some sort. A peppy young MC moderated with the help of a microphone that was turned to the highest setting, rendering his words almost unintelligible. The bags were checked to make sure no one had augmented with sand, then placed on a bathroom scale, the weight of each one noted on a piece of paper by a pretty assistant. Next to the table that held the scale, a poster, displayed on an easel, depicted two open hands, with a waterfall flowing from one to the other, and the dove of peace silhouetted against the waterfall. As we passed by, the children hopped up and down in excitement. Three days later, six bags of plastic still remained, their contents spilling out over the dunes.

Sofia, an elderly neighbor whose house sits just across from ours, describes Soliman Plage in the early days, when she and her husband bought their property in the 1970's. This area had become sought after for its pristine beaches, its quiet town, and its lack of tourists; a perfect vacation spot for city dwellers of a certain station, an echelon of society with some money at their disposal and a good deal of education- the understated elite, ministers and mid-ranked officials. The sand was like white powder, she recounts with disdain, the water crystal clear, the people took care of their houses, and were considerate of one another. Then it came, one hand washing another, bribes and corruption, and the boardwalk which had been planned between the first row of houses and the beach, gave way to a new first row, and then another. Because of the tides, barriers were erected at a prescribed distance from the houses to diminish the possibility of erosion. Because of the barriers, algae, seaweed and natural sponges, small, brown discs perfect for exfoliation, tend to accumulate on the shore

In the years since we built our house, the mayor, who used to live just at the entrance to the beach, has moved away, and the little store around the corner is shuttered after the owners divorced. Cows roam freely through the unpaved streets and can often be found sunning on the beach in the early morning, five or six gathered together. At night, the barking of wild dogs competes with that of purebred bull mastiffs and German shepherds, a recent acquisition for Tunisians, who traditionally don't abide by animals of any kind in the home. The beasts protect their families from the rooftops, and from ours we see our neighbor's dog, a water dish, and a small shelter for shade. Bones and feces pepper the area. The dog whines in greeting when she sees us, and the kids have taken to throwing her crusts of bread and pieces of beef salami from our roof terrace. One summer her teats are heavy, and in the afternoons, three roly-poly puppies make their appearance, tumbling about in the blazing sun.

We are the third row of houses from the beach, though 'row' is something of a misnomer. There is nothing strictly organized about the placement of the houses. Though the streets are marked, they bend this way and that, without traffic lights or stop signs. The distance from our garden gate to the sea is just long enough to make footwear an imperative. Besides, there is often broken glass. One has to be careful. On the beach, a makeshift soccer field is scanned for glass by the players before every pickup game. The boys, once they had grown a bit, joined in with pleasure, bringing home a new Tunisian phrase with every match. And sometimes yes, a cut from a piece of glass, buried deep in the sand. Once the foot had been cleaned and bandaged, the fear and pain quieted, a sense of pride and ownership, of initiation and strength followed. Their animation in the retelling of the incident underscored my hunch that maybe the degree of effort and worry we expend back home trying to protect our kids, might be misguided.

Over time, the residents of Soliman Plage have gradually morphed into an interesting mix of year-round residents, expatriated Tunisians returning with their families for the summer, European retirees living on a budget, and mixed couples - Tunisian and Dutch, Tunisian and Belgian, Tunisian and German - settling in a quiet, out of the way place. And it is quiet. We are near Hammamet, a place that became a destination spot known for its pristine beaches and then became overdeveloped. Waves of tourism brought groups of French, then groups of Germans, then groups of Russians, and, lately, Algerians to the area. Big hotels, all-inclusive, offer everything from water-skiing and camel rides to music and partying at night, or '*animation*', as they call it.

None of that reaches us at Soliman Plage, thankfully. I have yet to spot a tourist. Everyone here has some deeper connection to Tunisia, even the retired French sailor and his wife, who return to France a couple of times a year to visit their daughter and to bring back wine, assorted cheeses and thinly sliced ham. When he worked as a sailor on the big freightliners, Tunis was his favorite port and with the exchange rate, they can live like kings on a modest pension. Aside from the families who have homes here, the easy commute from Tunis brings tenting families every summer. Makeshift shelters, artfully cobbled together from poles, *kilim* rugs, blankets and sheets, create cozy, cool interiors for a weekend at the beach. A *darbuka, canoun*, and tea kettle offer entertainment and refreshment all day long. Sometimes the distant sounds of drumming and singing can be heard deep into the night.

Not all of the families end up coming back. Oftentimes the kids grow up and have little interest in returning to the country of their forefathers. We bought our property from a gentleman who had emigrated from Tunisia to Belgium. He had begun construction on the house, thinking to bring his family for vacations until he could retire here. As the kids grew older they wanted nothing to do with it. Discouraged, he put it on the market, not fully built, for a song. An architect friend helped us draw up plans and, brick by brick, we had it built over the course of a few years. I promised the kids we would spend our first summer there once the toilets were operational, and so we did, bringing over a container of Ikea mattresses and unassembled dressers, an old piano, an exercise bicycle, and the biggest dining room table we could find, complete with chairs. No TV, but Ali soon found an old radio, reminiscent of his youth, and promptly started collecting them. Years later, we now have four radios, but still no

TV, or internet, though we could set it up if we wanted.

Building continues in the town, and the summer is busy enough. A few blocks down, the town square is lively at night. Vendors sell *crêpes*, or *bambalone* (deep fried dough rings, dipped in sugar), or pizza, or *klub* (roasted sunflower seeds) in rolled newsprint cones. The cafés are busy, with customers vying for dozens of tables. The waiters can barely keep up as families add chairs to their tables. Children run around, brown from their day at the beach and refreshed from a shower and the requisite siesta. They weave in and out among the tables, chasing each other, begging their parents for an ice cream or a soda, occasionally falling or getting lost and seeking the comfort of a generous and sympathetic lap.

During one of our summers there, Tunisia is in the running for the soccer world cup. For an event like that, even those with a TV at home prefer to come to the square, where a small set broadcasts the game from the café counter facing the square. Tables are pushed to the side and chairs lined up for viewing. Shots of black, sweet coffee, mint green tea, sodas, *klub*, cigarettes, or *houka* are ordered excitedly. Waiters scurry to fill the orders so that they, too, can catch some of the game. The nighttime air is sweet and soft, the punishing intensity of the sun now put to rest. The scents of jasmine, mint, tobacco, coffee, and cologne waft along cool breezes brought in by the nearby sea. But the fans, mostly young men, are full of heat, shouting and cursing at the small screen as nearly invisible players run back and forth across the soccer field. Waves of loudly expressed disappointment echo through the square as players miss their mark, and when a goal is made, everyone cries in excitement and shoots to their feet, arms wide open, fists raised high.

The day after, the square is empty. Everything shuttered, save for the small store that sells all of the basic necessities for just a little bit more than what you pay in town. If you don't have a car, you go to town in a taxi, which congregate here in the square to take passengers in the morning. This is how we meet our friend, Abdel Islem, the taxi driver.

Most mornings, Ali and I go to market together, stopping at a café for a *capucin* and a *houka*. We are later than most Tunisians, arriving just before the market closes for the midday meal and siesta. The waiter at our café knows us by now and brings our order with a mere nod of the head. By the end of our first summer, Ali has forged relationships with a number of people in the market: the man who sells soaked chickpeas by the cup, for example, and the one who sells big bunches of mint and parsley, wetting them in a bucket of water periodically. Both of these men are blind, and, like Ali's father, work every day without assistance. We have 'our' fruit vendor, poultry shop, kefir and ricotta maker, bodega for odds and ends. There is a bicycle repair man on the corner, and he has fixed our four bicycles as the boys and their cousins use and abuse them. His small son is frequently with him, sitting obediently on a small chair in the entryway while his father changes tires, replaces chains. We frequent a certain bakery, even though the owner is often rude and impatient. His bread is good, and hot when we pick it up.

On one of our trips, Ali strikes up a conversation with the taxi driver, a young father in his thirties. Despite a disability, he gets out to open my door and help me out, he lifts our heavy market baskets into the trunk. He drives deftly and without hesitation, his left arm leaning on the windowsill, as his right hand seamlessly maneuvers the wheel, gear, radio, and gestures while he speaks. Over time, we will come to know each other, as he becomes another guardian angel of the house, taking care of the gardening and painting chores in our absence, supplying his young family with extra income. His wife, too, will visit when we are there, with her children, always bringing a favorite meal, or another plant for the garden. She is a school teacher in town, but hails from a farming family and has the indefatigable energy and generous laugh of someone who has grown up in the country.

Nights are generally quiet in Soliman Plage once the swallows have finished their evening dance in the dimming sky. Kitchen and garden sounds mingle with the gentle whisper of the nearby sea, or the muffled conversation of a couple returning from the square. Occasionally though, there is a wedding, and then the neighborhood becomes a party. Everyone knows about it, so everyone is invited, and everyone comes. The house of the bride fills with well-wishers streaming in and out. Sweet almond or strawberry drinks are passed around in tiny glasses, nut pastries with powdered sugar are served on shiny trays. The bride sits in a brocade chair, rented for the occasion, decked out in a battleship of a dress, also rented, hair and makeup professionally done, unrecognizable to her loved ones. Months of hard-earned salary have gone into this night. Neighbors and friends celebrate in concentric circles around the family, ululating intermittently and at key moments, as when the groom finally arrives, heralded by a cacophonous brass band, to take his bride to her new home in a sleek, beribboned car,.

Despite its detractions, Soliman Plage is paradise to me. In our summer house, hardly anyone rises before eleven, and so I have the place all to myself until they wake up. A house full of breathing, dreaming loved ones is a beautiful thing, and I feel them with me while I prepare my breakfast and take it out to the porch, still in shade in the early morning. Sometimes I will go to the beach for a swim, but not typically. This is the perfect time to write, or think, or settle into a good book. After a while, Ali and the children will come down the stairs, one by one, brown and sleep-soaked, looking for milky sweet coffee and buttered toast with quince jam. Another day begins, adventures await.

SUMMER'S END

Our last day in Tunisia. The season has begun to shift. There's a freshness in the air, and the sea is sometimes a few degrees cooler, making a warm, dry towel an absolute necessity in the evenings. I will think of our time here and remember a series of pictures, suspended moments. I will miss the simplicity of things - one kind of bread, milk, eggs, seasonal fruits and vegetables, one kind of soap, useful for everything. Even hairstyles are uniform, the men mostly clean-shaven with hair cut short, the women with long hair tied back, eyebrows shaped to resemble birds' wings.

What will the kids remember I wonder? Will they have noticed the same things I did? The plastic water bottles refilled with water every night and put in the freezer or used to drum along the gates of garden walls? Those same bottles carried the water to wash sandy feet after the beach. They also helped make deep, deep holes in the sand, and served as temporary aquariums for small, silver fish, excitedly caught in the sea and then returned.

I bet they noticed, the boys especially, that construction sites here consist of piles of sand and rock, a simple pulley suspended from a 4x4, a frayed nylon rope with a rusty hook, and a few men, exhausted and burnt, wearing sandals and straw hats and denim blue jackets, moving continually but never fast. Perhaps this is why the houses here have no basements. Backhoes and jackhammers, cranes, pneumatic lifts, are used only for the construction of huge glass and steel buildings, foreign banks mostly, in the city.

They will remember the fishing, and the little boy whose success with a bamboo cane, a three-pronged hook and a loaf of stale bread greatly surpassed their own with our Target fishing sets. Aicha will remember the night she prepared ten kilos of almond pastries with her aunts in the kitchen, rolling the almond dough into little sugary balls that smelled of orange blossoms.

They will remember, I hope, the very important ritual of kissing everyone upon entering or leaving a house, the fear and awkwardness in the beginning and the ease and delight by the end of the summer. Years later I will hear them giggle when they recount their great uncle's scratchy beard and peculiar odor, his warm hugs and tender heart.

They will remember the people we saw in the street, some unhinged by mental imbalance or circumstance, and hopefully also the fact that passersby would stop to listen to their ravings, look at them, laugh good naturedly, and give them something to eat. At home we learn to ignore the misfortunate, to avert our eyes, afraid of contagion or violence.

The dead kittens in alleyways they will surely remember, and the countless ones we rescued and nurtured and found homes for. The six-week old homeless puppy who followed Ali home one night, the dozens of ticks we plucked from his round belly, the hoops we jumped through to bring him home, to no avail. Salambo was his name.

The boys have learned how to light a *houka* and, despite my admonitions, how to smoke it. All of the kids have learned how to crack *klub* - sunflower seeds - between their teeth, sitting in front of the house late on a summer's night, and to sweep up the hulls after the last chair has gone back inside.

They have learned and felt, I hope, that life is in the living of simple moments, shared laughter and tears as well as arguments, that many hands make light work, that delight and adventure are everywhere if you are willing to look, that communication is more than language, that kindness is the greatest commodity, and that acceptance can be a form of strength. They have learned that strange might not be so strange if you stay with it awhile.

COOKING TUNISIAN

Cooking Tunisian food well depends upon many variables, some of which can be difficult to control. To begin with, it helps to have hardworking people with an appetite who have expressed a desire for a specific dish at some point in the last few days. It also helps if those people share sensual, visceral memories of that dish with the cook, and if they have the same mother. If this is not the case, preparations may be fraught with tension, and the eating is likely to be tinged with a faint aroma of disappointment. Perhaps this is why Tunisian families nearly always eat together, and always at home, and why they rarely accept invitations from acquaintances or friends not related by cooking. Perhaps this is also why, even in the wealthier circles, people tend not to eat out, unless they are getting pizza, or a roasted chicken, something neutral and generally enjoyed more by the children than by the adults. The restaurants, with their quadrilingual menus, are strictly populated by tourists. When I have gone out to eat with Tunisians, the meal has been peppered with criticism and we have often ended up in heated dispute with the manager.

So, we cook at home. Ideally, the cook is plural - a small gaggle of two to four sisters with their children. They have determined the meal of the day over a last, leisurely cup of coffee that morning, once the men and school-bound children have left the house in a state more fitting for quiet reflection. One, sometimes two, main dishes are decided upon after some discussion, taking into account the aforementioned appetites and whatever leftovers are lingering in the refrigerator. The rest is up to God, as manifested in the limitations of the purse, the quality and price of whatever is available at the market, and the moods of the vendors on any given day. Each woman knows, in the same way she knows her own pulse or the rhythm of her child's voice, which fruits and vegetables are in season throughout the year. There is rarely anything else available at the market, unless it comes from far away, which makes it pricey, past its prime, and generally regarded as suspicious.

The midday meal, the most important of the day, typically consists of two main dishes and a salad, with fresh fruit for dessert. Copious amounts of bread, French-style baguettes, are purchased at the end of the market run, with larger hands smacking at the smaller ones as they sneak into the *coffa* to break off the ends.

When they return home, the women seamlessly and without discussion fall into their habitual tasks: this one puts away the groceries, that one tends to the little ones' needs, the other cleans the fish or cuts up the chicken, and still another washes the fruits and vegetables, selecting them for size or ripeness to be used now or kept for later. Now and then, conversations arise; a question about the food, a remembered bit of news about a neighbor, a taste of freshly cut cucumber, or a hissed insult for the merchant who managed to sneak in a spoiled tomato or two. The one who stirs the sauce is the head chef, as it were. This is something unanimously and wordlessly agreed upon in each generation, but ritual deference includes offering a taste for approval to whoever is the self-appointed head of everything else.

Therefore, as you can see, the preparation is so complex and on so many levels, that cooking Tunisian food anywhere else, under any other circumstances, presents a formidable challenge. The only people I know who have done it successfully are my husband, cooking for a clientele of cherished regulars at our restaurant, and a friend of ours, who bears the nickname 'Godfather,' most likely due to his penchant for fine leather shoes and tinted eyeglasses. Godfather emigrated from Tunisia to the United States in the seventies. A butcher by profession, he had no trouble finding work. After his marriage ended, he spent his remaining thirty years in NYC as a bachelor, living in a one-bedroom walk-up on the Upper East Side.

Now he lives on an olive farm he purchased in Tunisia for his retirement, but even when we visited him in his tiny apartment, he would regale us with a Tunisian meal: *mirmez* or *macroona tunsiya* or whole fish, slathered in cumin and garlic and roasted to perfection in the broiler. Olives were always offered in abundance, along with home-pickled lemons and cold water after we had finished our opener of scotch. As required, Godfather always served plenty of bread with the meal, and for dessert, ice-cold grapes or melon cut into sections. He ate this way always, preparing the next day's meal after work and using the fresh meat that was given to employees as a perk at the supermarket where he worked. What he ate for dinner had been prepared the night before and given time to settle into its full flavor.

His culinary habits haven't changed since his retirement. His shopping is done once a week, at the nearby village where his sister resides. There, the merchants let him pick out his own produce. And a visit to his sister includes the midday meal with her slight variations on the family theme. When I press him for specifics regarding his recipe for *mirmez*, he answers only with gestures, winks, and waves of the hand that no one but a Tunisian could understand. I am warmed by the compliment.

So desire, I suppose, is the main ingredient: the desire not only for food and its sustenance, but also for the experience of selecting the ingredients and of preparing them without hurry, with nostalgia for an intimate and messy family context, even if that context is temporarily inaccessible. Time must be slowed so that the senses can be present and active, aromas and flavors discerned with full acuity. The best meals are conjured without haste, in a quasi- meditative state. Measurements of grams or tablespoons are hardly as relevant as the recalled image of a mother or aunt rounding her hand to make a cup or taking two pinches of salt with four fingers this time, instead of three. Even baking, that precise science, seems to happen more by the alchemy of pouring and stirring. I have yet to see a measuring cup or flour scale, at least in the home. The measures of the recipes that follow, as I have written them, are only approximations, very general guides for the variations you will discover on your own through tasting and trying, over and over again.

So, with these recipes, may I suggest that you try them out with friends or relatives, tasting as you go, adding a touch more of this, eliminating that altogether. Allow a few hours - no, a full day - for shopping, chatting, preparing, stirring. and tasting. Allow time for a coffee break and a rest. And then enjoy the food in good company, leaving not less than three hours for the meal. Clean up together. That way no one is left out of the conversation, which will have taken many turns through the course of the evening and which will leave a sweet aftertaste in the heart of every guest for a long time to come.

SIMPLE BITES AND SALADS

TUNISIENNE ASSIETTE OR SANDWICH TUNISIENNE

This is the perfect, easy summer dish, quick and refreshing. It can be infinitely expanded to accommodate unexpected guests if you have an extra tuna, eggs, and French bread.

INGREDIENTS:
- 2-4 leaves romaine lettuce, thinly chopped
- 2 eggs, soft boiled
- 1 5oz can tuna in olive oil
- 1 medium potato, boiled and peeled
- ¼ medium onion, chopped or sliced finely
- ½ cucumber, peeled, quartered and sliced thinly
- 1 plum tomato, quartered and cut small
- 1 Tbsp capers
- ¼ limoun* finely chopped
- harissa* to taste
- olive oil to taste

DIRECTIONS:

Distribute potato, cucumber, onion and tomato evenly on a bed of romaine. Use a generous-sized plate.

Add tuna and break up into smaller pieces, distribute evenly and drizzle with oil from can.

Add capers and *limoun*, scattered evenly.

Add *harissa* in dollops as desired.

Remove eggs from shell and add on top.

Drizzle with olive oil as desired.

Serve with warm bread. In Tunisia, everyone eats with their fingers (hands washed before and after dinner), using pieces of bread to catch the food. This requires some practice, but it's fun to learn if you don't mind getting messy. A well-bred Tunisian, my sister in law tells me, can be recognized among other things by how she eats. She uses only the thumb and the first 2 fingers of her right hand. And only ever has to lick her thumb! Bon appetit!

FOR THE SANDWICH:

Take one third of a fresh *baguette*, slice through the middle. Spread *harissa* as desired directly on the bread. Drizzle a little olive oil, if desired.

Layer the remaining ingredients (less is more) as desired.

For the sandwich, eggs should be hard boiled and sliced or left out completely.

Wrap up and bring to the beach. Don't forget to bring plenty of napkins and watermelon wedges for dessert.

*recipes in subsequent pages

BRIK OR SWEBA FATIMA

Brik are a favorite Tunisian treat, present at every celebration. They are relatively easy to make, and a delight for all ages and persuasions. Essentially you can take any leftover meats or fish and combine them with potatoes, parsley, and egg to make the sweba Fatima (Fatima's fingers), a Tunisian equivalent of the Chinese egg roll. However, though different varieties of brik have been attempted, the classic is the best, made with tuna and one barely cooked egg.

INGREDIENTS:

feuilles de brik (large, round phyllo sheets)
1 5oz can tuna in olive oil or leftover cooked chicken
raw eggs, 1 for each brik
2-3 cooked and peeled potatoes
4-5 sprigs of parsley, rinsed and finely chopped
half a medium onion, peeled and finely chopped
¼ - ½ cup of capers, drained
salt and pepper to taste
vegetable oil for frying

DIRECTIONS:

Separate the *feuilles de brik* and stack them loosely on a large plate. For *sweba Fatima*, you will need to cut the *feuilles de brik* in half, for *brik* you leave them whole. Line a second plate with paper towels to absorb the excess oil of the finished product.

For **sweba Fatima**, mix the tuna or chicken pieces with the onion, parsley, lightly mashed potatoes and capers, plus 2 eggs. Season to taste with salt and pepper and mix again.

Place about 2 tablespoons of the mixture an inch below the straight border of the half-circle of *feuille de brik*. Fold the straight edge over the mixture, then fold in the sides and roll the contents down toward the round edge, tucking the sides in as you go. The end product should resemble an egg roll. The ends can be sealed with a damp finger.

Heat about 2 inches or 5 cm of oil in the deep-frying pan.

Gently place the *sweba Fatima* - you should be able to fit 5 or 6 in the pan - in the hot oil and monitor carefully. If they are browning too quickly, turn the heat down. When one side is brown, turn them gently, being mindful not to splash. At no point should water come near the hot oil, as this can cause the oil to spit and burn your skin. When they are a nice golden brown, gently remove them from the oil and place them on the paper towel-covered plate to drain.

If you are making **brik**, mix the tuna or chicken with the onion, parsley, and capers and place a generous spoonful in the middle of the circle. Remember that in this case, the *feuilles de brik* are left whole. Just before you place it in the oil, crack one raw egg onto the tuna and deftly lift the ends of the *brik*, laying it gently on its side in the oil. This takes a little bit of finesse. Generally, you can only cook one at a time. Just as with the *sweba Fatima*, you want to turn the *brik* over once the first side is an even golden color. Ideally, the rim of the *brik* will be crisp and the egg still runny. Make sure you have plenty of napkins on hand!

Burghur

Burghur is a Tunisian winter soup, served on afternoons when the sky has been grey for days and the damp cold from the tiled floors in the house seems to rise like steam through the shlekas and into the bones. Ideally, a morning spent in the hammam with sisters precedes the meal-- and a siesta under a pile of blankets follows.

INGREDIENTS:
- 1 cup bulghur wheat, rinsed
- 1 cup chickpeas, soaked and half-cooked, or 1 16oz can, drained and rinsed
- 1 6oz can tomato paste
- 1 medium yellow onion
- 6-8 cloves garlic, coarsely chopped
- 4-6 stalks celery, with leaves
- chicken parts (2 wings and neck are sufficient for taste, more if you want pieces of chicken in the burgher),. A half-pound of stew meat (lamb or beef) can also be substituted.
- harissa or red pepper flakes
- 1 Tbsp turmeric
- 1 Tbsp ground cumin
- 3-4 bay leaves
- a few sprigs of parsley, rinsed and coarsely chopped
- olive oil
- salt and pepper to taste

DIRECTIONS:

If you are using stew meat, sauté this first in a small amount of oil in a heavy stew pot and remove

Sauté onions, bay leaves, and turmeric in about ½ cup olive oil

Add tomato paste and stir until color and consistency start to change, add some water if it starts to stick. It will bubble and break up a bit. Don't let it burn!

Add 2 quarts water, stir and bring to a boil

Add meat or chicken parts, bulghur wheat, celery, and half-cooked chickpeas (if you're using the canned chickpeas, add them later—see below), stir again and bring to a rolling boil. Lower the heat to medium and then let everything simmer until the meat and chickpeas are soft, about half an hour, adding water as needed if the soup becomes too thick. The oil should rise to the surface of the soup.

If you are using canned chick peas, add them in the last 5 minutes or so.

Before serving, add fresh parsley, finely chopped garlic if desired, and cumin. Stir to incorporate.

Add salt and pepper to taste

Serve with French bread and *harissa* on the side.

LEBLEBI

A pauper's soup, this is one of those dishes that serves for any meal. Any town square will have a leblebi vendor, with the traditional brown ceramic bowls stacked high. It sustains and cures everything from the common cold to a hangover. Many different items can be added, including tuna, harissa, capers or beef hooves, but the essential soup is made from chickpeas and garlic, with plenty of stale bread on hand to pile in and soak up the broth.

INGREDIENTS:

For the soup:
½ lb. or 1 kilo dried chickpeas - or -
2 12oz cans of chick peas
1 or 2 cloves of garlic, depending on your taste
½ teaspoon baking soda
salt and pepper to taste
1 piece of stale baguette per person

Possible toppings:
Tuna
Soft boiled eggs, 1 or 2 for each guest
Capers, drained and rinsed
Red wine vinegar
Olive oil
Cumin
Harissa

DIRECTIONS:

If you are using dried chickpeas, rinse them and soak them in a pot of water overnight or for 6-8 hours. Drain and rinse them, then put them back in the pot with abut twice as much water as peas. Cook them until nearly done, about 1-1½ hours, then add the garlic, peeled and slightly smashed, and ½ teaspoon of baking soda. Continue cooking until soft. If you use canned chickpeas, drain, rinse and put them in a pot with fresh water, about twice as much as the chickpeas, and continue as above. Season with salt and pepper. Before serving, add cumin as desired.

Ladle some hot soup into a generous-sized bowl, one for each guest. Top with whatever suits from the ingredients available. Give a good shake of the cumin, a dash of vinegar and some olive oil and serve with stale bread, cut or torn into bite-sized pieces. Mine has to have *harissa*. It adds a smoky quality that is just heaven.

OMUK HOURIA

INGREDIENTS:
- 2 medium-sized yellow onions, peeled and diced
- 1 lb. or 500g carrots, peeled and cut into small discs
- 2-3 cloves garlic, peeled and minced
- ground coriander or cumin
- salt and pepper
- approximately 6 Tbsps olive oil
- approximately 2 Tbsps red wine vinegar
- approximately 1 Tbsp harissa paste

DIRECTIONS:

Sauté onions in 2 tbsp. olive oil until soft.

Add carrots and enough water to cover the carrots.

Bring to a boil. Cook until soft. Drain the water and save it.

Thin the harissa paste with about ½ cup cooking water from the carrots.

Combine minced garlic, coriander **or** cumin, oil and vinegar, and harissa mixture. Add salt and pepper to taste. Mix well. Taste and adjust if necessary. There should be a balance between the spices where no single flavor dominates.

The coriander will yield very different results from the cumin. You should try each version. I prefer the cumin. In some families it is also customary to mash the carrots with a potato ricer or a fork before mixing them with the dressing.

Add the dressing to the carrots and mix well. Taste again. The sweetness of the carrots and onions should set off the spices just beautifully. This dish can be eaten room temperature or cold. It should not be eaten warm or hot. Mix again just before serving. Serves 6-8, approximately.

SHAKSHOUKA

INGREDIENTS:

**2-3 medium-sized potatoes, peeled and cut into thin, small
slices and soaked in water.**
2 heaping tablespoons of tomato paste
4-6 ripe plum tomatoes
2 Italian green peppers, cut into bite-sized pieces.
6-8 large eggs
3-4 cloves of garlic, peeled
1 Tbsp ground coriander
sea salt
ground black pepper
olive oil
harissa

DIRECTIONS:

Drain potatoes and sauté in hot pan, in about 3 tbsp of oil, until coated and heated through. Add tomato paste, reduce flame to medium, and stir until color and texture begin to change. Add 1 cup of water, stir, and increase heat to bring to a boil.

Pound garlic, coriander and a generous pinch of salt in the *meherez* until well mashed. Add all this to the tomato broth. Add fresh tomatoes and peppers and cook on medium heat until all ingredients are soft and incorporated. Add *harissa* and black pepper to taste, then the eggs, cracking them directly into the sauce and stirring gently with a wooden spoon as they cook. You are aiming for a texture somewhere between egg drop soup and scrambled eggs, with fibers throughout and appetizing chunks. The color should be a deep, rich scarlet, and the fragrance of garlic and coriander prominent throughout the house.

n.b. Depending on your family's definition, on whether your recipe is more influenced by Moroccan tradition or Tunisian, on whether or not you include potatoes, this may dish may be referred to as 'heja'. As with many things, I was unable to get a consensus among the different members of my Tunisian family.

Slata Fahkous

This is the quintessential summer salad in Tunisia. You can find varieties of this all over the Mediterranean – Greece and Turkey come to mind - but the Tunisian version chops the vegetables into tiny, tiny cubes (this is the daughter-in-law's test of refinement!) and adds mint to enhance the refreshing quality of this dish. Many children who will not eat salad will love this one, especially if they can eat it with lots of fresh baguette! While making the salad, the spears of cucumber often disappear mysteriously, so if you have little hands around, maybe prepare an additional cucumber or two.

Ingredients:
- 2 medium sized cucumbers
- 2 green bell peppers
- 2 tomatoes
- 1 medium sized onion
- 1-2 Tbsp dried mint
- olive oil
- red wine vinegar to taste
- salt and pepper to taste

Directions:

Wash, peel, and seed the cucumbers. Wash and seed the tomatoes and peppers. Peel the onion. Chop everything in little cubes - the smaller the better. Add the mint and dress to taste with the oil and vinegar, salt and pepper. Less is more on the vinegar. Toss well and serve with bread, and some nice, fresh *ricotta salata* on the side.

SLATA MISCHOUIA

Literally "grilled salad," this dish is much like the charred salsa you find in Mexico. You use a combination of hot and sweet peppers, depending on your heat tolerance, and add an onion and a tomato for additional flavor. This recipe takes a slow day and one during which you might not mind a little heat. The entire house will fill with the smell of roasting peppers and your efforts will be rewarded by the rich aromatic flavors of the final result.

INGREDIENTS:
2 hot peppers: poblano, jalapeño, or whatever is available.
1-2 sweet green bell peppers
1 medium onion
1 medium ripe plum tomato
olive oil and salt to taste

Serve with:
fresh bread
tuna
olives

DIRECTIONS:
Set the stove flame on medium, or use a grill. If you are using a charcoal grill, let the flames die out and start when the coals are glowing. If you are at the stove, you will need a grill accessory that allows the flames to come close to the fruit. Enclose the grilled vegetables as they are cooling, in a bowl, covered in plastic wrap, or in a lidded pot. In Tunisia, a plastic shopping bag will do, hanging from one handle on a drawer knob or hook.

Place the peppers, onion, and tomato on the grill and turn when one side becomes charred. Keep checking and turning until each piece is blackened. As the peppers become cooked, place them in the plastic bag.

Once you have finished and the peppers have cooled, take them out with gloved hands (dishwashing gloves are best to protect your skin). Peel the onion, and peel and seed the peppers and the tomato.

Finely chop each pepper or pound it with the *meherez*. Once everything has been processed, add salt to taste and a generous amount of olive oil. Serve with a nice dollop of canned tuna and a plate of olives. And, of course, fresh bread!

Tagine

Unlike the Moroccan stew-like tagine, the Tunisian 'tagine' is like a frittata, a baked omelet of sorts. It can be served warm or cold and goes nicely as an accompaniment to soup or salad for a light meal. Leftover cooked meats, beans, cooked vegetables, cooked pasta, or cooked potatoes can be incorporated at will. The basic recipe stays the same.

INGREDIENTS:

12 eggs, beaten
½ bunch parsley, washed and coarsely chopped
1 onion, finely chopped and sautéed
1 cup grated cheese - gruyère, parmesan, cheddar, or Mexican
    blend cheese will do
salt and pepper to taste

DIRECTIONS:

Preheat oven to 400 degrees. Mix all ingredients together. Grease a 9x9 baking dish. If you have leftover meats or vegetables, put them in the baking dish first. Pour the egg mixture into the dish. Redistribute as needed for evenness. Place the dish on middle rack and bake for 20 minutes. Reduce heat to 350 and bake for another 40 mins or until top is golden and a knife inserted in middle comes out clean. Cut into squares. Enjoy!

MAIN COURSES

BATATA ZAHRA

This was my children's favorite summer dish, simple to make and abundant. Enough liquid ensures extra sauce to pour over the potatoes, which they would mash with a fork on their plate. It goes well with the slata fahkous, and is best served outdoors on the patio under the bougainvillea and jasmine vines...

INGREDIENTS:

- 4-6 medium Yukon gold potatoes, peeled, rinsed and cut into quarters lengthwise
- 1 small chicken, cut into parts and skinned, rinsed
- 4 plum tomatoes, cut into quarters lengthwise
- 2 medium lemons, halved and juiced
- 2 medium onions, peeled and cut into quarters lengthwise
- 4 Italian peppers, whole, or 2 Italian and 2 jalapeño peppers, left whole
- ½ cup olive oil
- 1-2 Tbsp ground turmeric
- 2-3 cups water
- salt and pepper to taste

DIRECTIONS:

Preheat oven to 400 degrees.

Mix all ingredients together in a large mixing bowl, including juice from the lemons and their skins.

Taste liquid for spices, adjust as necessary.

Arrange everything in a 10x14 inch baking dish, taking care to distribute all the ingredients so that the dish looks pleasing to the eye and will cook evenly. The liquid should cover the ingredients at least half-way up.

Cover with aluminum foil and center in the hot oven. Bake

for 20 minutes.

Remove foil and reduce temp to 350, bake another 20 minutes or until chicken is browned and potatoes are done.

Serve directly from the baking dish.

Serve with French bread.

Couscous Tunsi

In contrast to Moroccan couscous, which is generally made with chicken broth and seasoned with ginger, the Tunisian version uses tomato broth and turmeric, a nod perhaps to its Roman heritage. The recipe I have included here allows for substitutions ad infinitum: lamb can be substituted for the chicken, or you could use a firm fish, like mullet or whiting, though the fish would be added at the end so as not to overcook the more delicate flesh. Vegetables can be exchanged to a degree, depending on what is available seasonally, though potatoes and chick peas are obligatory.

INGREDIENTS:
    1 lb. (500g) chicken parts, or a half-chicken, skinned, cut into
        pieces, and rinsed
    1 6oz can tomato paste
    bay leaves
    olive oil
    2 Tbsp ground turmeric
    2 Tbsp sweet paprika
    salt and pepper to taste
    3 medium carrots, peeled, rinsed, and cut into finger length
        pieces, then halved if thick.
    1 medium turnip washed and cut into 4 or 6 wedges.
    3 medium yellow-fleshed potatoes, peeled, rinsed, and cut into
        quarters lengthwise.
    2 stalks of celery, rinsed, and cut in half.
    2 medium-sized yellow onions peeled and diced.
    2 medium-sized yellow or green zucchini, rinsed and cut in
        half both ways.
    200g calabasa squash, or ½ butternut squash, washed, seeded
        and cut in half both ways—leave the peel on.

3 or 4 anaheim or similar chile peppers, rinsed and left whole, including stem.

6 mini red and yellow bell peppers, if desired, rinsed and left whole.

500 g or 2 cups cooked chick peas, drained.

500 g or 1lb. *couscous*, the finest grain available.

1 pat of butter

DIRECTIONS:

Sauté onions in ¼ cup of olive oil in a six quart, heavy-bottomed stock pot over a medium flame until translucent. Add chicken parts, browning to seal in the juices. Lamb shoulder can be substituted, but in either case the meat should be moved as little as possible, only turning when one side has browned.

Add oil if necessary and then the bay leaves, turmeric, and tomato paste, stirring briskly until the paste has changed in color and texture. Adjust the flame or add olive oil as needed to prevent the mixture from burning and sticking to the pot.

Add 2 quarts water, stir, and bring to a boil.

Once the sauce is boiling, you will add vegetables according to their cooking time, beginning with those which take longest: carrots, turnips, celery first, then potatoes and squash, ending with peppers. Check the meat periodically for doneness. Remove the potatoes when they are done so that they don't dissolve, and also remove any other vegetables that risk becoming overdone. Add the chickpeas last.

In a separate, large serving bowl, mix the dry *couscous* with a tablespoon of olive oil, a pat of butter, and salt and pepper to taste. Add a cup of boiling water and mix briskly with a fork, then cover with plastic wrap and allow to sit for 5 minutes. Uncover and add about 1 cup of the strained sauce, stir and cover again for another 3 minutes. Fluff with a fork and shape into a mound. With a slotted spoon or tongs, gently remove the meat and vegetables and arrange around the center in a decorative fashion. Serve the chili peppers on a separate plate for those who want them and reserve a gravy boat of the strained sauce for anyone who wants their *couscous* juicy!

Traditionally, the lamb *couscous* is made in winter, the fish in summer, the chicken anytime. For the fish, the carrots are omitted, and the whole fish cleaned and cut in half across the belly. The fish is added at the end, and cooked for a few minutes only, until just done.

Couscous royal is with lamb, and *merguez*, spicy lamb sausages, which have been grilled separately and added on top of the finished *couscous*.

Couscous is made from semolina, like pasta, and is usually available in grocery stores in the medium grain. Freshly-made couscous has to be steamed in the *couscousière*, a two-tiered pot in which the sauce cooks below and the grain steams above in a colander-like pot that sits above the other and is covered. If you have one of these pots, the commercially available couscous grain can also be steamed in this way.

Couscous is an obligatory dish in any celebration and should look inviting as such. Make sure the vegetables don't get overdone and give extra attention to arrange them as beautifully as possible.

HOUT MISCHOUI

Grilled or broiled fresh fish, Tunisian style.

INGREDIENTS:

**1 fresh fish per person: dorado, branzino, or other bluefish,
about ¾ pound each.**
1 tsp powdered cumin per fish
2 cloves fresh garlic per fish
½ tsp sea salt per fish

DIRECTIONS:

Clean the fish, leaving on heads and tails

Pound garlic, salt and cumin together, rub this paste in and
on the fish

Grill or broil for 2 or 3 minutes on each side, DO NOT
OVERCOOK.

*Serve with salads, homemade French fries, and fresh bread. Eat
with your hands, and don't forget to give the fish heads to the aunties!*

JILBENNA

INGREDIENTS:

1 lb. trimmed veal shoulder, cubed
1 lb. frozen petite peas
1 can artichoke hearts, unseasoned, or a ½ lb. frozen
1 medium onion, peeled and diced
2 medium sized carrots, peeled and cut into thick wheels
1 red pepper, seeded and cut into strips
2-3 jalapeño peppers (optional), rinsed and left whole
olive oil, ¼ - ⅓ cup
2 Tbsp ground turmeric
pinch of saffron (optional)
salt and pepper to taste

DIRECTIONS:

In a heavy-bottomed stew pot, sauté onions, turmeric and veal in a generous amount of olive oil (about ¼-⅓ cup). When the onions are soft and the meat just beginning to brown, add enough water to cover the meat (about 1 liter) and cover the pot.

Bring to a boil, add carrots, and cook on a medium flame until meat is tender. Add peas, artichokes, and peppers (jalapenos, too, if using), adding water to cover the vegetables if necessary, raise the heat and cover the pot. Bring to a boil and reduce heat to medium, simmering until vegetables are just done (5-10 minutes) and have not lost their color. Remove the jalapeños carefully so as not to break them and serve them separately for those who like it hot! Add salt and pepper to taste - don't be shy. The stew should have a kind of sweetness to it, and is a delight to look at, with its golden sauce with bright dashes of color from the vegetables. As always, serve with copious amounts of fresh *baguette*, and maybe a simple escarole salad.

KEFTEJI

INGREDIENTS:

> 6-8 medium potatoes, peeled
>
> 200-300g calabasa squash, or one medium butternut squash, peeled and seeded
>
> 6-8 italian peppers, rinsed and dried, stem removed, then seeded and left whole
>
> 6-8 ripe plum tomatoes, rinsed and dried
>
> half a bunch of parsley, washed and coarsely chopped
>
> half a red or white onion, peeled and finely chopped
>
> 2 cups vegetable oil for frying
>
> salt and pepper to taste

DIRECTIONS:

Cut the potatoes and squash into thin bite-sized slices. Heat the oil in a heavy-bottomed, large frying pan until a trial potato slice makes 'tsisch!' when you drop it in the oil. Reduce the heat to medium. Begin by frying the potatoes in batches, removing them to a large bowl as soon as they are golden and done through. Next, fry the squash in batches, adding them to the potatoes in the bowl. These will cook more quickly. Next, cook the peppers, and last the tomatoes. With the tomatoes, you will need to cover the pan as they cook, because they release water, which will cause the frying oil to pop and sizzle.

When everything is done and in the bowl together, Take 2 knives and scissor-cross them through the *kefteji* again and again to chop the ingredients into smaller pieces and incorporate them together. Add salt and pepper to taste. Garnish with a generous heap of chopped onions and parsley when you serve.

Kefteji should always be served room temperature, ideally with a nice, fried fish like mackerel or sardines.

LOUBIA

This dish is a nice hearty stew, served and eaten with French bread.

INGREDIENTS:

- 1 lb. ground beef, 85% lean
- 1 6oz can tomato paste
- 1 cup cannellini beans, soaked overnight and cooked, or 1 13oz can, drained and rinsed
- 2 medium onions, peeled and finely chopped
- 5 cloves garlic, coarsely chopped
- 1 head parsley, rinsed and finely chopped
- Plus another half a bunch of parsley, rinsed and finely chopped, for garnish
- 1 cup bread crumbs
- 1 egg
- olive oil, ¼ cup
- 3-4 bay leaves
- 1 Tbsp turmeric
- *tebeul**, salt and pepper to taste
- ½ pound of frozen or fresh spinach, thawed or blanched, drained and squeezed of excess water

DIRECTIONS:

Mix ground beef, bread crumbs, spinach, parsley, one half of the chopped onion, egg, *tebeul*, salt and pepper together.

Knead well and form into 1½ inch balls

In a heavy stew pot, sauté the remaining onions, bay leaves, turmeric and garlic in about ¼ cup olive oil until onions are soft

Add tomato paste and stir on medium heat until color and consistency begin to change. Add water if mixture begins to stick

- don't let it burn!

Add 1 quart of water, stir well, cover and bring to a rolling boil.

Gently place meatballs into boiling sauce. Cover and reduce to medium heat.

Cook for about half an hour to 45 minutes, adding water if it begins to look too dry, tilting the lid so it's partly open to reduce if there's too much liquid. It should have the consistency of a nice thick spaghetti sauce. The oil should rise to the top of the sauce.

Add beans in the last 5-10 minutes.

Add salt and pepper to taste. Garnish with a sprinkle of parsley.

Serve with copious amounts of French bread. Make sure everyone gets the same number of meat balls!

recipes in subsequent pages

MAKROUNA TUNSIYA

INGREDIENTS:
- 1 head garlic, peeled, smashed and chopped
- 1 12oz can tomato paste
- 2 lbs. beef stew or veal shoulder stew
- 4 medium Yukon potatoes, washed
- 1 green pepper
- 2 hot peppers
- 1 12oz can chickpeas, drained and rinsed
- 1 lb. ditalini pasta
- 4 or 5 bay leaves
- olive oil
- salt and pepper to taste

DIRECTIONS:

Sauté together garlic, tomato paste, and bay leaves on medium heat, stirring so that it doesn't burn.

Add 4-5 cups water, stir.

When sauce boils, add stew meat and cover.

Add whole potatoes and peppers and remove from sauce when done.

Continue to simmer over medium heat until the meat is tender and the liquid reduced by half.

Add chickpeas

Cook pasta separately in salted water with 3-4 bay leaves added

Drain pasta and add enough sauce so that pasta is lightly but evenly coated, add olive oil if needed.

Arrange in a serving dish. Start by cutting cooked potatoes in quarters lengthwise and slice the cooked green peppers, removing the seeds. Arrange the potatoes with the green pepper slices atop the pasta. Serve the hot peppers separately for those who want them or have *harissa* on the side.

Ali used to tell me you had to reduce the sauce until you could see a little lake of tomatoey oil on the top. The sauce will be thick, and when mixed with the pasta, it will seem a little dry. But it's one of those dishes you can't stop eating, even when, despite strict instructions not to, the aunties used *harissa* in the sauce and made the children squeal!

MIRMEZ

INGREDIENTS:

1 lb. lamb shoulder, cut into 3" pieces
1 cup dry chick peas, or 1 15-oz. can, drained
1 6oz can tomato paste
4-8 cloves garlic, slightly crushed
3 medium yellow onions, peeled, halved and sliced in strips
2 medium fresh tomatoes, seeded and quartered
¼ - ½ cup olive oil
2 - 6 Tbsp *harissa*
Salt and pepper to taste

DIRECTIONS:

If using dried chickpeas, soak them for 8 hours or overnight.

Sauté the garlic cloves and lamb in ¼ cup or more of olive oil until lightly browned.

Add tomato paste and a little water if necessary, stir for a minute or two until tomato paste changes consistency.

Add soaked and rinsed chickpeas (canned go in later) and water to cover, stir until well incorporated, bring to a boil.

Cover, reduce to medium heat, and cook for 1 hour, stirring periodically and adding water if necessary. Meat should be tender and chick peas slightly underdone.

Add onions and fresh tomatoes.

Cook for another ½ hour or so, until onions are soft.

If using canned chick peas, toss in during the last 5 minutes.

Add salt and pepper to taste.

Serve with bread.

Tunisian Rice or Rooz Djerbi

Tunisian rice was always a favorite at our little restaurant, though the cooking method was somewhat different from the traditional one. The traditional method uses a couscousière and, though the preparation is not more labor intensive, it does require a longer cooking time. This method, by steam, slowly fills the house with irresistible aromas. As Ali says, "you have to cook it until it smells just right".

Ingredients:

500g or 1 lb. lamb shoulder, trimmed and cut into 1" cubes
2 medium yellow onions, peeled and coarsely chopped
1 can of chick peas, approximately 500g, drained and rinsed
1 cup dried mint, crushed
500g or 1 lb. white rice, rinsed
½ - ¾ cup vegetable oil
500-700g or 1lb. fresh baby spinach, coarsely chopped.
Salt and pepper to taste

Directions:

Mix all ingredients, except for the spinach and starting with ½ cup of oil, thoroughly in a large bowl using clean hands. Add more oil if it feels dry.

Add spinach and mix gently until evenly incorporated.

Fill the bottom pot of a *couscousière* half full with water. Put the rice mixture in the top half and cover. Cook over medium heat for 45 minutes, uncover and turn the mixture gently and evenly, replace cover. Check water level in bottom half, adding water if necessary and continue cooking 30-45 minutes or until meat is tender. Serve warm, with a side of *harissa*. Serve in deep plates and eat with a soup spoon!

CONDIMENTS, DESSERTS

Harissa

This is the spicy Tunisian condiment that is served with every dish and also served as an appetizer with bread and a dish of olives.

INGREDIENTS:
500 grams dried red hot peppers (habanero are good)
3 small heads of garlic
1 Tbsp coriander or caraway seeds (adjust to taste)
Salt to taste

DIRECTIONS:

Soak the dried peppers in water overnight until soft. Drain.

Process peppers in a Moulinex or food processor until a paste is formed.

Peel the garlic and mash in *meherez* (mortar and pestle) with salt (or in a food processor).

Add the garlic mash to the pepper paste and mix well.

Add seeds, if desired, and salt and mix.

Serve with olive oil.

Conserve in glass mason jar covered with a layer of olive oil. *Harissa* will keep for a couple of months.

LIMOUN (PICKLED LEMONS)

Chopped up , these are an excellent addition, to any salad or sand-wich, giving all foods an unexpected brightness. Meyer lemons are best. The pickled lemons will keep in the fridge for months in the brine.

INGREDIENTS:
   4-6 meyer lemons
   sea salt
   1 raw egg in an unbroken shell
   1 mason jar with lid

DIRECTIONS:
   Wash the lemons with mild soap, rinse well.

   Trim the stem end.

   Cut each lemon in quarters about ⅔ of the way through. The lemons should look like flowers with 4 petals. Place a pinch of salt inside each lemon.

   Wash and rinse the mason jar and lid. Fill the mason jar ⅔ full with warm, filtered water.

   Add about a half-cup of salt, and stir until dissolved.

   Gently place the whole egg into the salted water.

   The egg should float to surface.

   If it doesn't, remove the egg and add more salt. Repeat until the egg floats with an area the size of a quarter above the water.

   Remove the egg and add the lemons. They should be com-pletely submerged. You can squeeze them in if there's limited room.

   Close the jar and store it in a cool place for at least one month, turning every few days.

   To test to see if the lemon is ready, cut a piece off. The peel

and pith should be almost translucent.
Everything is eaten but the seeds.

Tebeul

Tebeul is Tunisia's garam masala, or herbes de Provence, a multi-purpose spice blend used mostly in stews, especially with meats with modest flavor. Each family makes its own, and so each tebeul is slightly different, reflecting the history and preferences of the family lineage. This is the basic recipe. Tweak according to taste.

INGREDIENTS:

Yields 4 pounds of *tebeul*:
1 lb. caraway seeds
1 lb. hot chili peppers
1 lb. garlic
¼ lb. salt

DIRECTIONS:

Pound garlic and salt in *meherez*

Wipe the peppers with a clean, dry cloth. Remove the stems and seeds.

Hand clean the caraway, removing any stones and sticks.

Mix everything together in a large bowl.

Spread the mixture out on a blanket in the sun, preferably in a courtyard with protection from wind.

Let dry 2-3 months.

Peppers become crumbly.

Bring to miller to grind.

In the absence of a wind-protected courtyard and miller, these whole spices can be purchased and ground in a spice or coffee grinder.

Use generally in stews with chicken or beef to add flavor.

POMEGRANATE SEEDS OR STRAWBERRIES WITH ATARCHEIYA

INGREDIENTS:

The seeds from 2 large pomegranates (in the winter), or a pint of strawberries (spring), cleaned and hulled
1-2 Tbsp granulated sugar
1-2 Tbsp *atarcheiya* (scented geranium water)

DIRECTIONS:

To peel the pomegranates, cut a sliver off of each end, and make four incisions, running from top to bottom, just as you would to peel an orange. Now you can break the pomegranate apart easily. Use light pressure to nudge the juicy seeds from their pith, taking care not to burst them with excessive force. This undertaking requires the same kind of patience as that used in coaxing knots from tangled yarn. I suggest working with the bowl in the sink, as some splattering may occur, and pomegranate juice stains a bright vermillion. You should have 3-4 cups pomegranate seeds when you are done.

Add sugar to taste and *atarcheiya*. A word about *atarcheiya*, *z'har* (orange blossom water), and rose water. These aromatic essences vary in potency, depending on where and how they are distilled. Proceed with caution. You want only the suggestion of the aroma. It should not overwhelm the taste of the fruit. When used in excess, these aromatic essences can make any dish taste like soap. They are somewhat difficult to come by. Look in international or specialty food stores or online.

Mix well, preferably with your fingers so as not to bruise the seeds. Let chill for an hour. Mix again just before serving. Serves 4, approximately.

GREEN TEA WITH MINT

Fill a quart saucepan with water, bring to a boil. Add 4 generous teaspoons loose green tea. As soon as it comes to a boil again, strain and discard the liquid, leaving the leaves in the saucepan. Add fresh water and bring to a boil again, then simmer for a few minutes, according to taste (longer=stronger).

Prepare a teapot with a bunch of fresh mint leaves. Prepare glasses with a sprig of fresh mint and/or toasted pignoli (pine) nuts. Pour the green tea into the teapot and let it steep for a few minutes. Add sugar to the teapot, or have it handy for guests to sweeten their tea individually. Tunisians like their tea sweet. Serve with biscuits or fruit in the late afternoon, when the house is just beginning to rouse from its siesta.

Acknowledgements

Many thanks to my Tunisian family who received me with open arms. Nana and Azizi must be mentioned here first, but also and especially Latifa, with whom I feel a special bond. Thanks to my children, for letting me write when they were young and not getting into mischief, and for listening to the same stories over and over again. Especial thanks to Khalil for his dedicated work on the formatting, as well as the beautiful artwork of the cover and illustrations. Thanks to editor Susan Bruck, and to the friends and family members who read and re-read portions of the book over the years.

CPSIA information can be obtained
at www.ICGtesting.com
Printed in the USA
LVHW111113070121
675553LV00006B/536

9 781735 703800